A street athlete at age six and a national participant at age sixteen, **Marianne Torbert** has played and studied play all her life. She is interested in the dynamic potential of play and its role in growth and development. She holds a Ph.D. in the Psychology of Human Movement from the University of Southern California and is a member of the graduate faculty of Temple University, Philadelphia.

To my mother,
who continues to grow with each year of life.

Follow Me

A Handbook of Movement Activities for Children

Marianne Torbert

A SPECTRUM BOOK

Prentice-Hall, Inc., Englewood Cliffs, N.J. 07632

Library of Congress Cataloging in Publication Data

Torbert, Marianne.
  Follow me.

  (A Spectrum Book)
  Includes index.
  1. Play—Psychological aspects.   2. Games.
  3. Child psychology.   4. Perceptual motor learning.
  I. Title.
  BF717.T67   649'.5   79-20778
  ISBN 0-13-322909-2
  ISBN 0-13-322891-6 pbk.

©1980 by Prentice-Hall, Inc., Englewood Cliffs, New Jersey 07632

Editorial/production supervision
and interior design by Donald Chanfrau
Cover illustration by April Stewart
Photography by Carol Sonstein
Illustrations by Laurie Simeone
Manufacturing buyer: Cathie Lenard

A SPECTRUM BOOK

10   9   8   7   6   5   4

Printed in the United States of America

PRENTICE-HALL INTERNATIONAL, INC., London
PRENTICE-HALL OF AUSTRALIA PTY. LIMITED, Sydney
PRENTICE-HALL OF CANADA, LTD., Toronto
PRENTICE-HALL OF INDIA PRIVATE LIMITED, New Delhi
PRENTICE-HALL OF JAPAN, INC., Tokyo
PRENTICE-HALL OF SOUTHEAST ASIA PTE. LTD., Singapore
WHITEHALL BOOKS LIMITED, Wellington, New Zealand

CONTENTS

PREFACE

It seems that each book is written with a flavor that represents the biases and commitments of its author. Certainly this book is no exception. I would like to share a few of these with you.

I am a teacher. Although most teachers teach with books, pencils, and paper, I teach and learn through play, a tool that has continued to win my utmost respect and fascination since toddlerhood.

Over the years I have discovered that play has certain very exciting potentials but that these can come to fruition only when those who direct or affect the play experience view play and players in certain ways. I have tried to evolve some parameters that might begin to clarify this particular view of play and players:

1. The players are the most important part of any play experience.
2. Children have needs.
3. Behavior may be an attempt to deal with unmet needs.
4. An individual's view of self, others, and the world can be affected by play experiences.
5. When skillfully planned, movement activities have the potential to meet important needs.
6. *Everyone* has the right to healthy, positive play experiences. It is our responsibility to find ways to make this type of play available to all.
7. We can become more sensitive to needs and more skillful at selecting, modifying, and/or creating movement activities to meet these needs.
8. Our present "play" activities need to be studied carefully in

relation to both their positive and negative effects upon participants.

It is hoped that you will continue to find excitement in using play as an effective tool, and through experience, gain a growing proficiency in the ability to select, modify, and create activities to meet children's needs.

THANKS

To the students, teachers, and administration of Germantown Friends School, and especially Ms. Bobbie Konover, who made the enclosed photographs possible

To Mr. Arthur Lewis for his supportive assistance

To those who have taught me—my friends, my students, my family, and some very special teachers

To those in the Department of Physical Education and College of HPERD, and especially the "Chicken Foot Child" of Temple University, for creating a special environment which allows for individual struggle, growth, and uniqueness in an atmosphere of caring, scholarship, and camaraderie

To a group of secretaries and receptionist who keep daily life in the front office alive and personal

Sincerely,
Marianne Torbert

Play may be fun, but it is also a serious business in childhood. During these hours the child steadily builds up his competence in dealing with the environment.

Dr. Robert W. White
Professor Emeritus
Department of Psychology
Harvard University

INTRODUCTION

WHY USE MOVEMENT ACTIVITIES?

Play is exciting and fun filled. Its elusive qualities draw and hold its participants' energies and concentration. There is virtually an inexhaustible supply of movement activities which are flexible and can be modified or progressively changed to meet specific group needs.

Movement activities are action based and observable. Not only the planner but also the participant is receiving immediate and constant evaluative feedback. Just as one learns muscular control through frequent and repetitive experiences, so may play be a tool to evaluate social interactions and to experience and deal with various emotional responses and personal feelings.

It has been my experience that well-planned play may increase a child's willingness to become involved, and in turn, more· "ready" for the experiences that follow. Activities that allow a child to solve a problem, make a viable decision, to feel personal success seem to increase a child's active efforts to cope and his or her willingness to take chances. This effect certainly goes beyond the historically acknowledged value of play as simply a means of letting off steam or reducing stress.

WHAT IS YOUR ROLE?

Those who direct or affect children's play have a vital role. The awareness of the children' needs, careful selection and perhaps modification of activities, and continuous observation and evaluation make the experience a positive one.

HOW CAN THIS BOOK HELP YOU?

Over one hundred movement activities and modifications have been included in this book. Each is presented and analyzed to increase your insight into how and why the activity can meet specific needs.

The following areas have been selected for specific consideration:

- perceptual motor development
- attention span and concentration
- listening skills
- release of tension and excessive energy
- self-control
- development of thinking processes
- reinforcement of learned information
- social growth
- physical abilities
- physical fitness

Because the activities are frequently effective in meeting more than one need, a complete analysis of each activity has been included. A "Comments and Suggestions" section has been included with each activity to help you avoid some pitfalls. The "Modifications" may help you create new versions of the basic games.

Supplementary information on locating additional activities to meet certain needs (Appendixes A and B), as well as a brief appendix on making play equipment cheaply (Appendix C), are included.

The index serves the dual purpose of providing page numbers and gives a breakdown by activity of the potential for growth in the areas listed above.

PERCEPTUAL
MOTOR
DEVELOPMENT

1

Just outside my window yesterday I heard the squeal of brakes as two cars successfully avoided collision, a collision that would have brought at least the crumbling of metal and could have resulted in human injury. Probably few people realize the important role perceptual motor development plays in every daily act we perform. We tend to take these complex abilities for granted and attribute them to luck or innate ability.

The perceptual motor process involves perceiving through a sensory system, integrating and interpreting the perceived information, motor planning, responding, evaluating based on feedback, and storing. Perceptual motor development is based upon maturation and numerous rich environmental experiences. Because of the latter, it is possible to affect the degree of development and increase perceptual abilities to help prevent serious injuries and heighten the joys that accompany moving well.

The activities on the following pages will allow you some initial work in this area. For those who wish to work more extensively with perceptual motor development note Appendix A, "61 Activities That Develop Perceptual Motor Skills," on p. 195 and see the Index.

Children form a large circle. On a signal all children must try to cross through the circle to the other side without touching one another.

This is an excellent preliminary to many other activities that involve moving in relation to others.

Perceptual motor development body awareness and control; spatial awareness (an awareness of space, relative distance, and relationships within space)

Attention span and concentration encouraged by involvement, moving, interaction, and challenge

Listening skills see humming modification

Release of tension and excessive energy moderately active opportunity to move, change of routine, and problem solving

Self-control both emotional and body control necessary to accomplish objective; problem solving as a process of controlling the environment and self

Development of thinking processes problem solving; estimating (judgment) and adapting

Social growth responsibility toward others (avoid bumping)

Physical abilities dodging; predicting and anticipating another's movement; motor planning

COMMENTS AND SUGGESTIONS

Elimination is not usually necessary in such activities. The challenge is sufficient, and the child who would be eliminated is

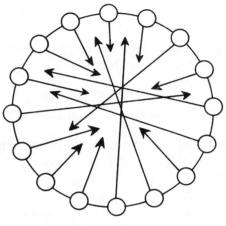

Figure 1–1

frequently the one who needs the most practice. If a child intentionally bumps another, *temporary* elimination (i.e., one or two turns missed) may help the child increase self-control; but remember this child needs an opportunity to practice developing self-control.

MODIFICATIONS

Use two lines rather than a circle. With all children moving in only two directions, the task becomes easier. Using a tight space, have children try to move in slow motion. Use different ways to travel: walk (forward/backward), crabwalk (see Figure 1–2), hop,

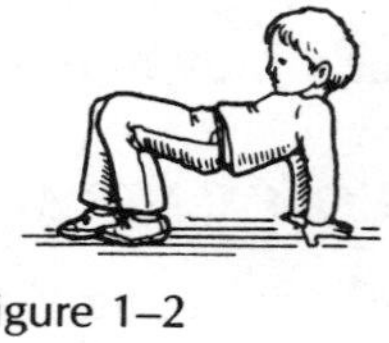

Figure 1–2

turn, and so on. Have children close eyes and hum. You might want only part of the group to go at a time, since you will need more space and some players to protect those who stray and to tell movers when to stop. This last modification is good preparation for "Robot," "Happy Landing," and "Car and Driver."

COWS AND DUCKS

Into each child's ear the leader whispers either "cow" or "duck." All children close their eyes and begin making the appropriate sound of the assigned animal. Like animals try to find each other.

Perceptual motor development body control; auditory acuity; auditory figure and ground discrimination (the ability to select a given stimulus from competing irrelevant background stimuli); auditory directional awareness

Listening skills awareness of direction and distance

Release of tension and excessive energy laughing; some silliness; movement

Self-control following directions, moving among but not into others, and staying with newly formed group.

Social growth responsibility toward group (to be careful of others); sense of belonging; unity and group solidarity (based upon having solved a common problem)

If there are many participants a child may help assign animals. A few volunteers to help the group avoid hazards or wandering off may be a good idea. This is also a good way to divide children into a particular number of groups for another activity. If you want more groups simply add more animal sounds.

MODIFICATIONS

Use more than two animals. Utilize sounds other than animal sounds (i.e., musical instruments, phonetic sounds, well-known songs, math problems and answers, spelling words, etc.). You might like to teach the children bird calls and play a similar game called "Birds." (Thanks to Schuylkill Valley Nature Center, Philadelphia, Pa.) A quiet version involves visual groupings. Animals are assigned, and each participant moves appropriately; like animals seek each other through visual rather than auditory clues.

MIRRORING

The leader demonstrates by facing the group and going through a series of moves in slow motion that the children are asked to duplicate *as* the leader moves. The children then take partners, facing each other and standing relatively close together. One child is to begin moving (leader) and the other to follow. After a period of experimentation, partners change roles.

Perceptual motor development body awareness; body image (awareness of body parts, their location, and relationship); body

control (balance, coordination, movement duplication); directionality (awareness of directional space and relationships—under,
over, behind, left, and so on); laterality (awareness that there are
two different sides to the body); motor planning (the ability to
organize a motor response); spatial awareness (estimation, relationships); temporal pace

Attention span and concentration continuous involvement;
sharing a challenge; clear and simple objectives

Release of tension and excessive energy challenge; change of
pace; moving and stretching

Self-control duplicating movement in *slow motion;* constant
self-evaluation

Development of thinking processes creating; careful visual
observation; translation; exact duplication of visual input

Social growth working with another and being responsible to
follow and to lead; being able to work without constant adult
supervision

Physical abilities body control

COMMENTS AND SUGGESTIONS

You might start the children by simply having them do any slow
motion they choose to see how very *slowly* they can move.
This is an excellent time to discover children who have difficulty
placing body parts in specific positions. This may be an indica-
tion that these children should be tested further for perceptual
motor difficulties, or they may need further simplification of the
progression. If children have difficulty with this activity, consider
"Follow Me."

MODIFICATIONS

Go from simple (only one body part moving) to complex (more than one body part moving at the same time).

Move to a count (pacing), with each new position taken on 1–2–3–4– or in "flow" (moving slowly and continuously from one position to another).

Have the children do this activity while sitting.

Have the children stand behind a leader and move as the leader moves ("Me and My Shadow"). This variation can include some traveling (i.e., forward, backward, etc.) (see also "Shadows").

FOLLOW ME

The leader stands facing the group and extends arms in a very specific (held) position. The children are asked to duplicate this position. The position is changed.

Perceptual motor development body awareness; body image; body and space relationships; directionality; laterality; visual discrimination; visual pattern recognition; motor planning; movement duplication; two-part body coordination

Attention span and concentration constant individual involvement; need for careful visual observation; challenge and pace

Released tension and excessive energy stretching; moving; change of routine

Self-control following another; following directions

Development of thinking processes monitoring and duplicating visual demonstrations

Physical abilities duplicating visual models

COMMENTS AND SUGGESTIONS

Activities such as this one are used in perceptual motor screening. This is a good activity for learning to observe any difficulties the children may be having. Children can check themselves for correctness of response by observing others. Self-correction may be preferable unless a child has no awareness of his or her errors. Even then you might like to have the children work with partners in an activity such as "Mirroring" before singling a child out for special individual work.

If you find children who seem to have consistent problems in reproducing patterns you might (1) try to determine why these children have problems (Do they have the same difficulty reproducing directional lines with paper and pencil? Do they simply need practice? Do they also reverse letters and numbers or confuse "b" with "d," "p" with "q," etc.?); (2) contact the reading specialist to see if further testing might be important and available; (3) study materials related to perceptual motor development. The position you take in relation to the children (mirror image) may be confusing to some of them. If this seems to be true have them stand behind you. If they can follow your movements, have them note how the group "mirrors" a leader facing them by duplicating left arm with right arm, etc. Some children could be having difficulty with the concept of mirror image rather than having any perceptual problem.

This type of activity can be used in a hospital as a challenge.

You may wish to begin by using only one arm (simplicity). If all children find this task simple add the other arm.

Simple patterns are those in which the arms are in similar positions (e.g., both arms straight out, both up diagonally from the body, etc.). You may wish to begin with these simple patterns and then add complexity by placing your arms at different levels. Straight arm movements are simpler than bent ones. Begin with the former; then if the group finds them simple, go to bent-arm positions.

Be creative.

You might wish to do this exercise in conjunction with "Show Me the Time" and "Mirroring."

Note "African Simon Says" and "Arrows."

BODY-BUILT LETTERS AND NUMBERS

Have the children try to form letters or numbers with their own bodies or with a partner. Then ask the children questions and have them try to answer by forming letters, words, or numbers.

Perceptual motor development body image; body awareness; body coordination; body and space relationships; motor planning; spatial awareness; pattern recognition

Self-control self-direction—must accept responsibility of deciding what to do

Development of thinking processes creative; thought-provoking; pattern recognition; problem solving

Reinforcement of learned information information most appropriately selected by leader

Social growth cooperation

COMMENTS AND SUGGESTIONS

Remember you may get many kinds of answers. Try to perceive how the children see their answer as a particular letter or word—which may also give you some important clues to specific difficulties.

If you are not sure that a particular answer is the one you are seeking, ask the children also to reply verbally as they do the exercise.

Sometimes children may have to lie on the floor to form letters or numerals.

If your group seems particularly to enjoy this type of activity, refer to Anne Green Gilbert's book, *Teaching the Three Rs* (Burgess Publishing Company, 1977). She has a multitude of suggestions for language arts, math, science, social studies, and art.

MODIFICATIONS

This activity can be used for answers in "True or False."

Try to find ways to modify this activity to reinforce various important concepts.

For older children, ask part of the group to form a basic word. Then have the observers modify the word (one or two letters at a time) by adding to it or replacing a letter with one of their own.

The children stretch material (blanket, canvas or parachute) on the floor. One child lies face up in the center of the cloth. The rest of the children slowly lift and stretch the cloth, raising the "riding" child off the floor. Holding the material at about waist level, the children gently and slowly move the rider up and down.

Perceptual motor development body awareness; kinesthetic awareness; body control (in flight); movement adaptability or adjustment; temporal awareness (preparation for "give" on landing and tensing on "send off"); body and space relationship

Attention span and concentration thrilling; elicits cooperation; allows child to be an "affector" (the cause of something that happens); team timing

Release of tension and excessive energy thrilling

Self-control being excited but still remaining in control; waiting for a turn; helping others enjoy an experience

Social growth trust; working as a team unit; helping another to enjoy a special experience; waiting for a turn; sharing; enjoying another enjoying something

Physical abilities body awareness and control; balance without a supporting surface

Physical fitness develops the shoulder girdle and muscles of the upper back

COMMENTS AND SUGGESTIONS

The material should be nonabrasive and strong enough to lift and hold any child in the group. Re-evaluate its strength each time you use it, as age and use can weaken the fabric.

After riders and lifters are experienced, you may wish to let the rider be lifted slightly off the cloth. Encourage a *gentle* lifting.

Riders should be allowed to volunteer. Some may choose not to ride, which is acceptable. Encourage but do not force participation as a rider. Watch for the child who might like to ride but is not assertive enough to demand an opportunity.

Girls wearing skirts or dresses can hold them to their sides as they ride.

The neck is a very vulnerable area of the body and should not be snapped. Encourage the children to tuck their chins as they "ride" off the cloth. Tell them not to stick their tongues between their teeth.

Thrilling experiences tend to refresh and contribute to sense of calm for some children.

MODIFICATIONS

With a circular material you can turn this activity into a merry-go-round ride.

With a parachute and older children, several individuals can be lifted on the merry-go-round at once. Feet are placed near the center of the parachute and remain on the floor. Bouncing is not advisable with more than one rider since the riders will tend to move together.

A "trust fall" can be fun for experienced and responsible children. A child (volunteer) stands on a *stable* elevation, such as a *firmly held* chair. The rest of the children hold two sides of the material at about chest height. The material may have to be rolled in from the sides to make a cot-like receiving surface. When all are ready, the child who will fall turns her or his back to the material and moves close to the edge of the supporting platform. Falling backwards, the child is caught gently. Then the children at the foot lower their end of the material and help the child to stand. Encourage the child who is falling to keep his or her body as straight as possible. Note: You may have to adjust the level of the receiving surface in relation to the height of your holders and that of the supporting elevation. Go cautiously at first.

CAN YOU DO THIS?

Children use a specific part of the body (i.e., head, elbow, foot, knee, shoulder, etc.) to spell or otherwise describe various phenomena selected by the teacher or leader.

Perceptual motor development could meet needs of children with specific problems in body and space relationships

Attention span and concentration constant new challenge without failure

Listening skills participation based on listening

Release of tension and excessive energy stretching; creating; being challenged; change of pace; moving

Development of thinking processes following the verbal statement; problem solving; generating individual solutions

Reinforcement of learned information can be adapted to reinforce learning

Physical abilities body control (balance; coordination)

EXAMPLES

Place your right elbow higher than your ear.
You have an imaginary piece of chalk on your left foot; write your name on an imaginary chalkboard [balance].
With your head write the answer to this problem: 3 is a fun one.
Put your left foot under your left hand and put both behind you.
Slowly circle each arm backwards three times [pacing, stretching chest muscles, counting, following directions].

COMMENTS AND SUGGESTIONS

This activity should be used and modified to meet a particular need, whereupon it becomes much more effective.
This activity might be used in conjunction with "Points and Parts."

MODIFICATIONS

These exercises can be used as quick challenges almost anywhere or anytime or in any number to change the pace or meet other needs.
They may be used after lunch to get the children into a listening mood before continuing their lessons. They can even be related to the upcoming lesson.

CREATIVE TEETER-TOTTER

The object is to construct progressively a multiple-part balancing teeter-totter of whatever boards, tires, etc. that are available. As it is being developed, all members of the group try to balance themselves on it as part of the creation. Balancing for a (slow) ten-second count, with no end of a board or part of a person touching the ground, is considered an official success.

Perceptual motor development body awareness; kinesthetic awareness (awareness of body, body part position, and balance made possible by a sensory system within the muscles); balancing (adapting); spatial awareness and seeing cause and effect relationships; estimation

Attention span and concentration being an affector (causing something to happen) and being affected; group problem solving; group challenge; sense of belonging to a functioning group; being needed for total success of group

Self-control working as a team to solve a specific, clear-cut, challenge, where all participants' efforts contribute to team success; patience and perserverance

Development of thinking processes perceiving purpose; creating; generating alternative solutions; problem solving; interactive planning; considering cause and effect; testing reality; evaluating

Social growth group cooperation and teamwork; listening to others' ideas; making contributions

Physical abilities balance, static and dynamic

Thanks to Phil Gerney of Cheltenham School District, Philadelphia, for this idea.
Check all materials for nails or other hazards.
This is a good time to take pictures.
If you happened to be studying balance, this activity could reinforce learned information. Perhaps a discussion of balance could appropriately follow this activity for your group.

MODIFICATIONS

For small children, one short two-by-four and one long two-by-four board could be used.
Two children could try to balance with each other by using a short two-by-four as a fulcrum and a three-foot-long two-by-four as the balancing board.
Balancing boards for individuals can be made up of a two-by-four approximately twenty to twenty-four inches long and a two-by-four fulcrum. To challenge children who can balance easily, have them try to turn the balancing board on the fulcrum or reverse their foot position on the board without losing their balance. Ask the children to create new challenges for themselves. Balancing with eyes closed is difficult but possible.

NORTH, EAST, SOUTH, AND WEST (ORIENTATION)

The children stand and face a given direction. The leader calls out a clue for a specific direction (e.g., "Where does the sun come up in the morning?" or "Face Europe"), and the children try to face in that direction.

Perceptual motor development reinforces awareness of location and orientation; helps in perceiving relationships

Attention span and concentration active involvement (must attend to be able to respond); moving

Listening skills oral clues (children can take later visual cues from others, especially if they do not know the answer, but since play is repetitive and tends to encourage players to challenge themselves, children frequently listen more carefully as trials continue to see if they can respond both more quickly and more independently)

Self-control continuous involvement and concentration; flow, group unity or pattern, and basic structure; success (you may want to plan for several successful trials interspersed with some difficult challenges)

Development of thinking processes understanding or interpreting questions, translating from one mode (knowing) to another (application), and making appropriate responses; immediate, direct feedback allows for self-evaluation

Reinforcement of learned information orientation and information about location (within a building or neighborhood; review of geography, map study, current events, etc.); lack of sufficient knowledge readily observable in child

COMMENTS AND SUGGESTIONS

Thanks to Wilma Chamberlain of Jacksonville, Illinois, for introducing me to this activity.

Since each child receives immediate feedback, it is usually not necessary to correct errors. Perhaps if children are allowed to correct their own errors immediately, more learning will occur.

If you wish children to commit themselves to their answer you can have them all give the answer at one time (following a countdown). Perhaps they could do so while balancing on one foot. You might encourage them to challenge themselves by balancing on a different foot each time since we tend to balance only on one side.

It might be helpful to have the children talk about why knowing directions is important.

MODIFICATIONS

Vary places and locations (e.g., directions of compass, countries, states, cities, neighborhood places, locations within the building or immediate vicinity).

Start with N–E–S–W signs on walls, later removing them to see if the children are learning.

Add aspects of physical fitness to the activity (e.g., "Turn north and run in place").

Ask compound questions, such as "Turn toward the state where the battle of the Alamo was fought." Children must know *both* the state and the direction to answer the question.

ATTENTION SPAN
AND
CONCENTRATION
2

Children are basically curious. A baby will play with a particular object for a considerable length of time and hang on to it tenaciously even as its attention is distracted to another object. But the baby's attention seems somewhat without direction or specific purpose other than the sensory stimulation it receives from whatever it is attending to.

We live in a world of sensory bombardment, and to interact effectively with it we must learn to separate the relevant from the irrelevant in a given situation. We must delineate purpose, perceive relationships, and from these draw conclusions upon which we can act. Thus, attending and focusing (concentrating) are two important skills. Our everyday functioning and the ability to learn effectively require these components, and we need to experience them to develop competence and skill.

Because the purpose of most movement activities is relatively clear, a child soon becomes aware that attending and focusing are vital to attaining the desired results. A child whose attention wanders usually becomes quickly aware of the effect and will have an almost immediate opportunity to adjust to more successful behavior.

As adults, we have found that telling a child to pay attention or concentrate does not usually help, but giving a child a meaningful reason for practicing these skills may prove more promising.

If this area is of specific interest, see the Index for additional activities that can be of help.

LUMEY STICKS

Each child makes two lumey sticks, roughly eight to twelve inches long and approximately an inch to an inch and a half in diameter (easily held in the player's hands). They can be readily made by rolling newspaper to selected size. (See "Making Equipment at Little or No Cost," p. 201.) Partners sit cross-legged facing each other or at a narrow table or desks pulled together. The sticks are moved in unison by partners to a count of three. The sticks are usually held as if one were holding a candle, about halfway between top and bottom. Usually two or three basic patterns are introduced (see below) and then children are encouraged to create their own sequences and patterns.

Perceptual motor development visual tracking (the ability to visually follow a moving object or person); visual figure and ground discrimination; object manipulation; eye, hand, and object coordination; patterning and sequencing; temporal patterning (perceiving time patterns, such as rhythm)

Attention span and concentration required to succeed and respond to partner; a moving object, rhythmic pace, and patterned movement; mental, physical, and social involvement

Self-control personal challenge; awareness of improvement; continuous involvement and focus; responsibility to another; teaches self-pacing

Development of thinking processes creative; problem solving; develops memory (pattern and sequence)

Social growth cooperating with another over an extended period of time

Physical abilities eye, hand, and object coordination

COMMENTS AND SUGGESTIONS

Basic Patterns:

1. Hit low end of sticks on ground; then hit two sticks together; then hit partner's right stick with your right stick. Repeat, but hit your left stick to partner's left stick.
2. Same sequence, except hit both partner's sticks on the third beat. Repeat.
3. Same sequence, except pass (toss) stick (right to right) to partner on count of three. Repeat tossing left to left.

One technique is to keep the sticks in an upright position on the toss, lifting them slightly in the air to give partner more time to toss and catch. When both sticks are being passed it may be best if one partner tosses to the inside and the other partner tosses to the outside. You may find it a more cooperative learning experience if you allow children.to work out these solutions or techniques for themselves.

Sticks can also be flipped to self, crossed, and so on. Perhaps the most innovative experience is to let the children create their own patterns, sequences, and techniques.

This chant can be used. Some leaders prefer not to introduce the chant too early; others choose to teach it before the activity, and some have recorded it on tape and played it in the background as the children worked with the beginning patterns.

Some believe this may have been an Indian game played with knives to maintain manual dexterity during the long winter months.

Movers sometimes use blank newsprint paper to wrap dishes. The local newspaper might also be willing to help you out. Since

1- 2 -3　1- 2 -3　1,2 - 3　1,2 - 3　1- 2 -3　1- 2 -3　1,2 - 3　1,2 - 3
MA CO WAY CO TAY O　WAY CU-EE　TAH NA　MA CO WAY CO TAY O　WAY CU-EE　TAH NA

Figure 2–1

newsprint does tend to come off on the hands, this unprinted paper is preferable.

Some leaders use wooden dowel rods for the lumey sticks. My experience has led me to believe that paper lumey sticks are quieter, safer, and easier to come by. Mothers tend to become upset when they discover that the length of their brooms or dust mops have been shortened 16 to 24 inches.

Lumey sticks is an activity that can be developed over several sessions. It can also be used for performances or demonstrations by groups or individuals.

MODIFICATIONS

Children can work individually in one large group, learning several basic patterns and the chant before working with a partner. With some groups this sequence would be preferable. Children can all sit in a circle. In this formation the children sit close together and pass to the person on their left or right. In this position a "standing stick" pass can be used. That is, a player tries to stand the stick (balanced) in a position directly in front of the receiver so that this player has time to pass his or her stick and grasp the new one. This activity requires skill and cooperation.

Various numbers of players can work together.

Tall sticks (24 to 36 inches long) are sometimes used (newspapers are rolled lenghwise). Here the stick is frequently balanced on its end ("standing stick") as it is passed. Children may choose to stand when using tall sticks, and groups of four, five, or six are frequently involved.

SWEDISH MEATBALL

Each player is asked to be sure he or she knows at least two other players' names (if group is new or if there is a new member of the group). They are also allowed to use the leader's name (if the leader is willing). The player with the ball throws it to another player and at the same time calls that person's name. That player then continues.

Perceptual motor development visual tracking; spatial awareness (estimation and relationships); eye, hand, and object coordination; directionality

Attention span and concentration unpredictable personal involvement, fast action, circular formation, and flying missile; being identified (being known and being "someone" may lead to increased, positive involvement)

Release of tension and excessive energy moderately active; choice of receiver; built-in challenge: can choose one's own level of risk (i.e., limited risk—call someone one is sure one knows; a little more risk—call a name just learned; big risk—call a name one is not really sure of; bigger risk—take a real chance at making a mistake or ask someone his or her name)

Development of thinking processes memory; minor decision making

Social growth learning names and identities; belonging; feeling comfortable with group; helping others feel more comfortable (being sure all are involved and making good throws)

Physical abilities lots of easy practice in throwing and catching

COMMENTS AND SUGGESTIONS

The use of a yarn ball (see "Making Equipment at Little or No Cost," p. 201,) rather than a regular ball is important: (1) a soft yarn ball tends to be an "equalizer" and is less apt to separate the skilled from the less skilled children; (2) it may help reduce the fear some children have of an oncoming object; and (3) it allows the game to be played almost anywhere (without damage). The group should be encouraged, as a team, to try to include all players *if* this does not occur automatically.

This is a good activity to help a teacher or leader learn the names of group members or to help a new child feel more comfortable in a new situation.

Even though you are encouraging total inclusion, a player should still be allowed to throw to whomever he or she wishes—which gives the uncertain child a degree of comfort. Also there is a bit of humor when two players choose to pass it back and forth rapidly to each other. This will usually last only a few throws and then they will pass it to someone else.

Throwers should be encouraged to *follow through* directly at their target. This is excellent practice and is important for improving accuracy for all activities.

This may be a good time to emphasize the responsibility of the thrower to give the receiver the best throw possible, since a miss is frequently the result of a bad throw rather than a poor catch. The thrower should follow through toward the center of the receiver's chest.

The thrower's willingness to take risks probably reflects his or her feelings of adequacy within the group.

MODIFICATIONS

If furniture cannot be moved, play the game from whatever formation is possible.

A circle formation allows everyone to see and be in easy throwing distance from everyone else.

Do not feel that you have to encourage speed. It will occur as the children become more skillful. Children find ways to challenge themselves as they feel comfortable and ready.

This activity might be a good preliminary to "Team Juggle."

MONSTER'S CHOICE

Children form groups of four. Each group has a monster ("it"), who designates who will be the "prey." All but the monster join hands and face into the center of the circle. When the signal is called, the monster tries to see how many times the "prey" can be tagged while the other three players try to prevent it. The monster is not allowed to reach into or across the circle. The leader calls "freeze" to stop the action. The remaining two players become the monster and the prey, and the leader begins play again. For the third round the original monster and prey can switch roles, and if the children have not tired of this activity, a switch can be made in the fourth round also.

Perceptual motor development balance; spatial awareness (estimation and relationships); body and space relationships (direction and laterality)

Attention span and concentration being hooked together; singleness of purpose; responsibility as part of a group; constant involvement and adaption

Release of tension and excessive energy vigorous activity

Self-control exciting; sense will of other two persons and make rapid decisions and compromises (some awareness of the effect of interaction—thus decisions are based on more than the repercussion to self)

Development of thinking processes adapting to a continuously changing situation

Reinforcement of learned information (1) guarding and protection technique (stay between offense and what is being guarded); bending knees for quick starts, stops, and balance

Social growth protecting and being protected; working with two others toward a common goal; compromise and give and take

Physical abilities agility; balance (adjustment to outside force); ability to stop and start quickly and absorb force

Physical fitness some shoulder girdle development; a good vigorous workout in limited space

COMMENTS AND SUGGESTIONS

If there are not even groups of four, the game can be played with a couple of groups of five, with four in the protective circle.
If the area available is limited, you may not be able to have all the children playing at once. If so, you could have them count "touches" for monsters.

In some cases you may wish to have the protected player designated in some way (e.g., strip of cloth around arm, headband,
hat, etc.).

Encourage a child to be honest when tagged, but also realize that
an excited child may truly not think a tag occurred. You may
want to avoid an overemphasis on the score.

To prevent groups from bumping into other groups, place an X
on the floor. If a group steps beyond this mark, it counts as a tag,
and the group must return to the original location on the X.

You may wish to teach the technique of using bent knees to
change directions quickly and maintain balance.

You may want to discuss briefly the idea of guarding (relate
"Monster's Choice" to basketball) by staying between offense and
goal.

MODIFICATIONS

A long strip of cloth could be tucked into the back of a waistband
and grabbed by the monster. This device is more evident than a
tag but does require time to replace after each successful snatch.

A monster could have the option of changing the prey at *any*
time by calling the name of a new prey.

Perhaps with very young children or those who have some
difficulty in spatial awareness, an adult could be the monster and
wear a halloween mask. The pace of the activity would need to
be determined and controlled by the adult. Excitement could
increase the effectiveness of the activity or destroy it.

SNATCH THE BACON

Divide the group into two even teams, which face each other.
Starting at opposite ends each team counts off, giving each child
a specific number. The leader then calls a number. The two

children having this number move quickly to the "bacon" (cloth, bicycle innnertube, etc.) which is halfway between the two teams. The objective is to try to snatch the bacon and run over the team line without being tagged by the other player. Crossing the team line or tagging the snatcher wins for that team.

Attention span and concentration challenging; competitive; enjoyable to watch; anticipating a turn

Listening skills remembering signals and listening for particular call

Development of thinking processes developing strategies

Physical abilities alertness; reading another's movement; possible reduction of reaction and movement time; agility

COMMENTS AND SUGGESTIONS

The "bacon" should be sufficiently large so that opponents will not bump heads when both snatch at the same time.
We may need to question the number of players doing nothing in this activity. Maybe it would be good on a hot day or when you feel children need to learn to be patient and wait their turn. Again, it depends upon your objective(s).
If those who have been called seem to be taking too long, you may wish to give a countdown, and if there is still no action, call that snatch a draw.
If a group is uneven, either the leader can play or the extra child can call the numbers. Be sure this child exchanges places with another periodically.
Having a card with numbers on it and crossing them off as you call them may insure that everyone has a turn.
Selecting a partner to divide the group into two even teams is a very fast and efficient method, but we might want to consider

the possible discomfort for the shy, unchosen, or awkward child. Counting off by twos or playing a game such as Cows and Ducks might be worth the extra time.

MODIFICATIONS

Call more than one player at a time.
Members from each team try to push or pull a large, stuffed laundry bag across their line (tagging is not a part of this modification). A large cageball or old mattress rolled up could also be used. Several numbers might be called at once, depending on the size of the "bacon" and the children.
Use an old bicycle tire tube for pulling ("Tire Tug").
Give math problems to determine the number of the snatcher.
Use a combination "Snatch the Carpet" (see "Carpet Activities").
Have a carpet strip for *each* snatcher. The called players go to a carpet, stand on it, and try to move it over a specified line as fast as possible. A child who has severe problems in mobility (e.g., cerebral palsy, Canadian crutches) might participate by merely touching the carpet and returning to his or her team goal line. Carpets might also prove helpful where space is limited.

DETECTIVE

One child (the detective) is asked to leave the room. A leader is selected. The leader begins a movement which all the other children also do. As the leader changes a given movement, so do all the other children. As soon as the children have the idea, the detective is invited back into the room. It is clarified that the detective's task is to discover in three guesses or fewer who is initiating the new movement.

Perceptual motor development visual awareness and discrimination; audio awareness and discrimination (see sound modification)

Attention span and concentration detecting source of change; staying alert to possible change

Listening skills audio awareness and discrimination; visual awareness and discrimination

Self-control concentrating and persevering; quickly adapting and blending into new movement; self-direction

Social growth accepting responsibility for and learning to function as part of a group with a common purpose

COMMENTS AND SUGGESTIONS

Being aware of audio and visual clues in one's environment is an important skill.
Try to encourage a variety of movements using different body parts.
If having the detective leave the room slows the activity down too much, simply ask him (or her) to turn his back on the group or close his eyes while a new leader is designated (by being pointed at). Have this player raise his or her hand so all the children can see who their new leader will be.
You might wish to have the children discuss strategies for concealing who is leading and those for detection.
If the children are mature and experienced in directing their own

play, you may wish to have more than one group functioning at the same time.
See "Where Is It"?

MODIFICATIONS

Movements can be all visual (more difficult to detect) or can include sounds, such as clapping, tapping, jumping, etc. (easier to detect). If the sound starts and ends quietly the change is harder to detect.

Movements can be big (easier) or as small (more difficult) as tapping a finger or wiggling a nose. One strategy is to start a movement very small, progressively increasing its size until it is quite large, and then reducing its size again. Anywhere in this process the movement can be modified or changed.

SOLITARY PING-PONG

Children each work individually at the task. The objective is to hit the ball in the air, trying to make it bounce on alternate sides of the modified Ping-Pong paddle (see Figure 2–2) as many times as possible without missing. The child keeps count. When a miss occurs, the count begins again. Each child tries to better his or her own record.

Perceptual motor development eye, hand, object coordination; visual tracking; spatial awareness; timing and rhythm

Attention span and concentration basis of activity

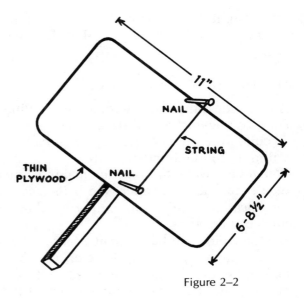

Figure 2–2

Self-control perseverence in face of some failure; competition with self and intrinsic self-evaluation

Development of thinking processes trial and error with feedback; analysis; problem solving; estimation of force and rebound angles

Physical abilities force and angle adjustment; fine motor control

COMMENTS AND SUGGESTIONS

You might want to stress competition with the children's personal previous score rather than with one another. This emphasis allows for more success and a continuous challenge for every child.

This might be a good activity for children with lower body limitations and may be useful in hospital recreation programs.

MODIFICATIONS

A child can simply hit, with a regular Ping-Pong paddle, a Ping-Pong ball against any vertical wall.

A child can bounce a Ping-Pong ball on a regulation paddle without modified net structure.

You might want to consider making nylon stocking and coat-hanger rackets and paper wad balls (see Appendix C). With this modification a child can simply hit the paper wad in the air to him- or herself.

For the child who has a great deal of difficulty with this activity, a ball (paper wad, whiffle, etc.) can be hung (tethered) from above. Let the child hit the object as it swings on the string. This swing pattern is much more consistent than the free-flying ball.

BIRDS FLY

All stand. A leader is selected, who quickly names various things that fly. Each time the leader names anything that flies the players all flap their arms vigorously (e.g., "ducks fly," "mosquitoes fly," etc.). If the leader names something that does not fly, all the children should cross their arms quickly across their chests. Anyone who flaps when he or she should have crossed arms, must sit down and continue participating from that position.

Attention span and concentration continuous involvement and decision making; frequent opportunity to move; verbal or visual input from other children

Listening skills basis of ability to make quick decisions

Release of tension and excessive energy opportunity to move and stretch (especially in the shoulders and upper back, which tend to be a location of tension)

Self-control involvement based on decision making and response, which require self-determination and direction

Development of thinking processes rapid decision making based on auditory input

Physical fitness shoulder girdle development

COMMENTS AND SUGGESTIONS

Before starting this activity you might want to talk about what flies and what doesn't so that the children can be leaders.
An adult or bright child who understands the concept of the activity probably should be the first leader.
This is a good quick exercise for restless children, giving them a chance to move.
Because the shoulders and back are sources of stress from sitting, it is helpful to exercise and stretch this area.
Those who have limited self-control will probably begin by taking the late but more obvious visual input from other children, but as the activity progresses, most children will be challenged by the independence allowed by the verbal input. Notice that those who fail are not eliminated but must sit and respond; thus

a child can still gain from the experience, but from a position that involves greater external control.

This might be a good preliminary activity to "Simon Says" (see below).

If you wish to encourage children to attend to auditory input you could ask them to close their eyes.

MODIFICATIONS

"Simon Says" is similar to "Birds Fly." The leader says, "Simon says stand up"; "Simon says reach high"; "clap hands." The participants are to do everything that Simon says, but if a direction is not preceded by the words "Simon says" (as in "clap hands"), it is not to be followed. See "African Simon Says."

SNATCH THE FLAG

All players tuck a cloth strip into their waistbands on the left hip. The object is to snatch other flags, at the same time trying to prevent one's own from being taken. Players may not touch their own flags nor hit or push another player. A child can only protect her or his own flag by moving so that it is out of a snatcher's reach.

After a halt is called the flags are returned to the players who have lost them. Play begins again on the leader's signal. This does not have to be played as an elimination game.

Perceptual motor development spatial awareness (estimation and relationships); body and space relationships; body control and coordination

Attention span and concentration basis of success; must also be able to shift and adjust attention and concentration rapidly

Release of tension and excessive energy rapid, vigorous movement; constant challenge

Self-control playing within the rules without becoming overly excited or angry

Development of thinking processes rapid monitoring of a changing environment; rapid decision making

Social growth playing within the limitations of the rules

Physical abilities alert visual input with rapid motor responses; agility; adaptability; moving (dynamic) balance; may reduce reaction and movement time (reaction time is measured from the recognition of stimulus to the initiation of movement; movement time is measured from the reaction to the completion of the task)

Physical fitness vigorous exercise

COMMENTS AND SUGGESTIONS

Adult leadership can be important.
Because this activity is potentially chaotic, you may want to seriously consider the best progression for your group (see modifications below).
My personal bias is that this activity should be used to encourage the development of social responsibility (safety) and skillfulness. Cloth strips are tucked in, not tied, to prevent torn clothes. If a player doesn't have a waistband, a long cloth strip can act as a belt into which the flag is tucked.

At least ten inches of flag should hang free for grabbing.

Be aware that flags on the floor are hazardous, although minimally outdoors.

Because this activity is so vigorous, you may need a whistle to halt the action.

The amount of time allowed for each episode can be changed. Too much excitement or fatigue can lead to an increase in injuries.

You may want to allow children to "buy out" and "buy in"; possibly a "rest" box could be established.

MODIFICATIONS

If space is limited you may want only part of the group to participate at a time.

Strips could be worn on both hips.

Two teams (two colors) can play. The players pull the other team's flags out, and teammates protect each other (more strategy and teamwork).

Two children could play against each other. To avoid bumping you may wish to limit space. Children can be assigned to a specific area, or each of the opposing players would have to hold one end of a third cloth strip.

Losing a flag could eliminate a player, but it doesn't have to. Elimination has both an advantage (reducing the number of players in a crowded space) and disadvantages (the difficulty of enforcement and the tendency to eliminate those who need involvement most).

You could include an individual "freeze" call by an official for unnecessary roughness or touching. A freeze could eliminate a player for that round. A "no touch" rule may reduce injuries and encourage greater skill in some groups.

You could create a scoring system or play without score. The challenge of the latter may be sufficient, and scoring may complicate the activity.

FOUR SQUARE

One child stands in each of the four squares (see Figure 2–3), and the ball is bounced from one to another in any order. The ball must be hit or pushed into a square other than the child's own and must bounce only once before being hit again by another player. This game can be played like "Infinity Beachball Volleyball," with each group of four seeing how long they can keep the ball going; or it can be played so that the player missing steps out, all members already in the squares step to the next highest numbered square available, and a new player steps into square 1. The object of this game would be to stay in as long as possible.

Perceptual motor development eye, hand, object coordination; visual tracking; spatial awareness

Attention span and concentration uncertainty and continuous involvement; desire to participate; pace; territorial protection (it is important to be able to maintain attention in situations in which direct involvement is uncertain and inconsistent)

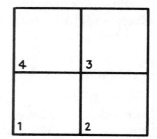

Figure 2–3

Release of tension and excessive energy change of routine; challenge; focus of attention; social and individual involvement

Self-control playing within rules; making appropriate decisions when questions arise; awaiting a turn; playing without the direct and constant supervision of an adult

Social growth functioning together with others without continuous adult supervision and when decisions go against oneself; being fair to self and others

Physical abilities eye, hand, object coordination

COMMENTS AND SUGGESTIONS

The size of the court depends on the children's sizes and abilities. A four-by-four-foot square might be a good start. The children can stand outside of the squares to play.
To help the children succeed, stress follow-through to where they wish the ball to go.
This is also a good playground activity, which children can play by themselves. You might wish to have several courts painted on the playground if this activity becomes popular. Then the children could choose between cooperative ("Infinity") and competitive "Four Square."
Challengers usually line up about four feet in back of court 1.
Rules should be established according to the skill of the children (see below).

MODIFICATIONS

Less skillful children could bounce and catch the ball.
More skillful children could hit the ball. At first, hitting it gently upward is easiest. Later, children may start hitting down which makes the ball go faster.

The difficulty may be increased by having players hit from one to another in a particular order or by declaring "line" balls out of bounds.

ZIG ZAG

The group forms a circle, with one player standing in the middle. Turning around, this player points to another player and says either "zig" or "zag." If zig is called, the player selected must name the player to his or her left before the challenger can count to ten. If zag, is called, the player on the right must be named. A miss means that the player changes places with the challenger.

Perceptual motor development auditory discrimination

Attention span and concentration waiting but remaining alert—a more difficult test of attention and concentration than continuous involvement

Listening skills quick interpretation of a verbal clue

Release of tension and excessive energy exciting; change of routine; dealing with *specific* and *time-limited* stress

Self-control functioning under stress

Development of thinking processes making quick and simple choice under stress and responding appropriately

COMMENTS AND SUGGESTIONS

If a count to ten is not sufficient time, have the challenger count "one thousand one, one thousand two . . . ."

Change positions of players to add new challenge. Players must now remember new names.

This activity may be helpful when a new child enters the group or when you are trying to learn names.

MODIFICATIONS

If "zig" and "zag" are too complicated, you might use "right" and "left."

The challenger calls zig and points to a player, who names player to his or her right, who names player to his or her right, etc., continuing around the circle as rapidly as possible until the challenger calls zag (reverse direction) or points to a new player and calls zig or zag.

LISTENING
SKILLS

3

Much of life is based upon auditory input and the appropriate responses to it. Awareness of and alertness to sound, the ability to discriminate among and identify sounds, to selectively listen to particular sounds, to recognize sound patterns, and to determine the direction from which a sound originates all serve important functions.

Children need to develop their listening skills, and certain movement activities can help them.

If this area is of particular interest, see the index for additional information.

CROWS AND CRANES

Divide the children in half (having even teams is not important). Have two lines face each other. One line is designated as "crows," the other as "cranes." The leader slowly announces "cr . . . ows" or "cr . . . anes." Those in the line called become the taggers, and the others try to avoid being tagged by moving to a designated safe area (usually beyond a specified line behind them). All those tagged join the other team, and the game continues.

Perceptual motor development discriminating sounds for accurate selection of physical response; body control under stress (see additional audio and visual modifications)

Attention span and concentration uncertainty and need to interpret important information

Listening skills recognizing differences among similar sound patterns

Release of tension and excessive energy excitement and running; laughing

Self-control rapid decision making and changing of excitation levels; many trials allow practice

Development of thinking processes interpreting information as rapidly as possible and making one of two possible decisions (limited choice)

Social growth belonging to a minimally organized team; being careful not to push another when tagging; becoming a "captured" member of another team (sometimes it is fun to be wanted in even little ways)

Physical abilities may reduce reaction time; body control

COMMENTS AND SUGGESTIONS

Two ways to divide a group in half quickly are (1) to have each child grab another, one going to one line and the other to the other line. You can even practice this technique with the children as a game: do even groups form? how quickly? You will want to stress the result rather than who chooses whom; (2) to have children count off by twos, sending ones to one line and twos to the other. You might want to have the children hold up one or two fingers as they are numbered—in case they forget the number. If lines are needed, masking tape can be used on the floor. An activity at the end of the day might be How Well Can We Get Up the Masking Tape? Masking tape usually sticks well.

Have a safe area clearly designated (do not use a wall if children are likely to run into it and be injured).

Giving the complete word very slowly can increase the suspense. You might also want to include other words, on which no one moves: crazy, crouch, crackers, crowd, etc.

If one team is very small, make them the taggers a couple of times in a row—which will give them a chance to increase the team size.

Outside, grass may be better than hard surfaces, and weather conditions may make a difference.

Have the children tag each other below the waist to prevent falls.

MODIFICATIONS

This game could be played in limited space or with the children seated facing each other. Arrange players so that a single step or a simple pull back would put them out of the tagger' reach. Players must think and react very quickly to avoid being tagged or to tag another. This version could also be used as a preliminary to the more active version.

This is a good playground game. The children will have to listen even more carefully outside. Running space should not be too great since it would increase injuries and decrease the number of calls.
Change the calls to stress other audio discrimination needs, e.g., ch–sh, words that begin with p or b, etc.
Modify the game to meet other needs, e.g., even versus uneven answers to math problems.
This could become a visually oriented game, and thereby include the deaf child, by having a signal that is seen rather than heard, such as an air-filled pillow with a different color on each side. The side that lands and stays upward determines the taggers.
See "Lion, Hunter, Gun."

SOUNDS LIKE

A volunteer stands so all can see and acts out a verb ending in -ing (such as hitting, dancing, rooting, docking, etc.). The other children try to interpret the action. If they believe they have the answer, they go to the moving child and whisper it in the child's ear. If it is correct they join the moving child, acting out another word that sounds like the original one. Each new clue should help the other children find the original word. When they believe they have the word, they whisper it in the first child's ear. If they are wrong, they may gather more clues and try again. Finally all or almost all will be moving.

Attention span and concentration problem solving; periodic addition of new clues may help

Listening skills pattern recognition and discrimination among sounds; similarities and differences in words that sound alike

Release of tension and excessive energy change of pace

Development of thinking processes use of clues in interpretation and decision making (the educated guess)

Reinforcement of learned information could be used in conjunction with learning to analyze sounds, words, and meanings

Social growth contributing; risking; active involvement

COMMENTS AND SUGGESTIONS

If you think your children will need help in understanding this game, you could use a preliminary one in which you give them a word and the group tries to see how many "sound alike" words they can list.

At the end of an episode you might have the group try to guess what some of the movers were doing.

If you find some children having a great deal of difficulty, you might quietly ask them some questions about what they think the various children are doing. Having the children involved allows you time to observe and give individual attention.

MODIFICATIONS

The leader gives a word. All the children try to find a word that sounds like it. As soon as they think they have one, they begin the action. Later, words are checked against the original word. The guessing child could select any moving player rather than only the original word player, whose word may still have him or her stumped.

WHERE IS IT?

The children form a circle. A container with an object in it that rattles is passed around the circle. The direction of the pass can be changed at any time at the discretion of the players. After a little practice passing the object, the players close their eyes and continue to play. At a signal from the leader everyone must stop. All players are asked to put their hands slowly behind their backs. The leader calls for eyes to be opened. Keeping one hand behind their back, players may indicate their desire to guess where the object is by raising their free hand. The Leader selects guessers. If the location is not guessed in three tries, the object is revealed and the game continues.

Perceptual motor development directional discrimination; body and space relationships

Attention span and concentration closed eyes; seeking clues; receiving object

Listening skills determining direction from which a sound comes

Self-control correctly interpreting one's environment

Social growth being fair and being trusted (not peeking)

COMMENTS AND SUGGESTIONS

The player with the object or those who just passed the object may guess someone else to fool the group.
If the rattle is not loud enough, ask each player to turn the container over as it is passed on.
See "Detective."

MODIFICATIONS

After the call of "stop," the object can be passed *quietly* two or more times as the leader counts 1–2–etc. Players try not to let the object rattle during these passes.

Instead of using a rattle, each player must say a quiet "beep" as he or she passes the object.

There can be more than one circle.

Two objects can be passed, and the groups must find both of them.

SOUNDS TO MOVE BY

Large movements in place, such as hopping on one foot, running in place, clapping, jumping with two feet, making large backward arm circles, slapping thighs, ˙rotating head (both˙ directions), circling hips (both directions), are matched to specific sounds. Examples (these may be difficult):

drum	train	saxaphone
spoons	bus	bluejay
sticks	motor boat	woodpecker
sandpaper block	oboe	mockingbird
bell	clarinet	frog
airplane	French horn	cricket
car	flute	

When the children hear a given sound they are to try to respond with the corresponding movement. For example, if the bell had been matched with running in place, then the children would run in place as the bell is rung. When the bell stops the children stop. When the next sound is heard the children move according to the matched movement.

Attention span and concentration challenge (difficult for some) to hear and do (if a child cannot get clues immediately from the sound input he or she can move according to the visual input from other children; thus a child can accept a challenge at more than one level)

Listening skills basis of activity

Release of tension and excessive energy allows choice of participating at different levels; respects and encourages challenge

Self-control making decisions about oneself (personal choice)

Development of thinking processes memory; recognizing sounds

Physical fitness depends on selection made by leader

COMMENTS AND SUGGESTIONS

If the environment is conducive to choice within the child's ability and we, as leaders, can be patient, children will seek growth and challenge (progressively) at *their* level. When a child is inattentive or out of control, factors beyond the immediate situation may be the cause, or the situation may be threatening rather than challenging. (A threatening environment is one in which the child has no choices at which he or she can succeed.) You may wish to start with fewer than five sounds and possibly add more later.

Having children all respond in movement allows them to learn from each other and allows you to check the correctness of their responses and observe their functioning.

At first it may help to put movement clues (drawings, pictures, etc.) somewhere where they can be checked by the children.
You may wish to have the children practice which movement goes with what sound.

MODIFICATIONS

After the children have learned the basic format of the activity and have begun to be familiar with which sound corresponds to what movement, you might add another challenge by encouraging them to close their eyes whenever possible—thus relying only on themselves and their ears. At first some children will need to keep their eyes open all or part of the time, but try to observe these children over several sessions to see their progress. Sounds can also be used to indicate directions the children are to move (e.g., sandpaper—to left; spoons—to right). Eyes are open for this version and the children should be at a fairly proficient level since errors are more serious (possibly one child bumping into another).

Visual clues rather than audio ones can be used.

Create your own version of this activity.

TIGER, TIGER, WHERE'S THE TIGER?

The leader asks four children to help by being tigers. The tigers are placed according to the ability of the participating group (may require some experimentation), and more skillful groups can have these tigers closer together. All other children close their eyes. The leader points to one tiger, who thereupon roars. The leader then asks, "Tiger, tiger, where's the tiger?" All children with eyes closed point in the direction from which they believe the roar came, and say "Tiger, tiger, there's the tiger." Eyes are opened and the tiger that roared raises her or his hand. This process is repeated.

Perceptual motor development directional discrimination of sound

Listening skills determining source of sound by locating the direction from which it comes

COMMENTS AND SUGGESTIONS

This might be a good opportunity to look for possible hearing difficulties.

Be sure to change tigers so that all the children can participate in the listening part of the activity.

If you are in a place where excessive noise is not going to bother anyone, you might like to allow the entire group to audition for the role of tiger. Have all the children roar at once (this always seems to let off a bit of steam). You can tease them a bit if you want by telling them that they will have to all do better if you are going to find a good tiger among them. You might have one group roar at another group.

MODIFICATIONS

Have the children meow very softly; this sound is more difficult to locate.

Have the tigers change their location in the room after the other children close their eyes.

Use only one tiger, moving as quietly as possible around the room (no roaring). When the children think they hear the prowling tiger, they call "Tiger, tiger, there's the tiger" and point in that direction. The tiger freezes, and all the children check their accuracy. A new tiger is chosen.

If several children all find the prowling tiger at once, you may select more than one prowling tiger for the next turn. Tigers not caught during a turn could continue to prowl during the next turn ("Prowling Tigers").

GESTURE NAME GAME

Each participant prepares large movements to represent her or his name. Each syllable of the first and last name has a separate move (although a move once used can be repeated). The first child starts: "Hello, I am *Bill Button*." The rest of the group responds, all doing the same moves, "Hello, *Bill But-ton*". As quickly as possible the next child takes his or her turn, and so on.

Perceptual motor development motor planning to duplicate audiovisual model; dealing with two interrelated and competing sensory inputs

Attention span and concentration learning to attend to audiovisual presentation *available only for a brief time;* immediate feedback and opportunity (next call) to recover attention

Listening skills matching audio with visual and reproducing both

Release of tension and excessive energy involvement; movement

Development of thinking processes careful observation; utilizing audio and visual input simultaneously; memory (short term and long term)

Reinforcement of learned information syllabication

Social growth identity; opportunity to lead and direct group; listening carefully to another

COMMENTS AND SUGGESTIONS

This activity and many others that encourage young children to work together can be found in Terry Orlick's excellent book, *Cooperative Sports and Games*, Pantheon Press, 1978.

This type of activity is helpful when a new child enters the group.

It also helps adults learn or review the children's names.

Asking for volunteers may be a good way to begin.

MODIFICATIONS

With some groups you may wish to use only first names.

If you have a large group, you might do a few names each day, repeating some of the ones already done as you move along. This could be a daily activity to reduce restlessness. Only doing a few names each day would also give some children an opportunity to think about what they would like to do.

You could have a challenge match after the children have given their names and movements. When you put your hand over a child's head, as many children as possible respond with that person's name and movement. With some groups you might prefer to give the children ten seconds or so to decide as a group. Then, on a signal from the leader, the entire group says the same and does the appropriate movement.

UNITY TURNS

The group stands and faces front. The leader gives signals for turns (e.g., quarter turn right; half turn left; about face; etc.), and the group tries to respond as rapidly as possible.

Perceptual motor development left and right discrimination; ability to move and stop quickly (body control); estimation of turning distance

Attention span and concentration pace; continuous involvement; uncertainty of happenings; individual needed for group effectiveness

Listening skills all information received auditorily

Release of tension and excessive energy involvement; movement; change of pace and routine

Self-control ability to follow instructions; seeing the effectiveness of group unity

Development of thinking processes ability to hear, interpret, and respond; mental alertness over a period of time

Social growth working together for the smooth functioning of the group; sense of belonging

Physical abilities pivoting; body control

COMMENTS AND SUGGESTIONS

This type of activity may help to increase group unity, depending on the leader's approach and attitude.

MODIFICATIONS

This activity can be turned into a game called "Streets and Alleys Tag." An "it," a runner, and a signal caller are selected. All other players form lines and rows; i.e., the players stand side by side (lines) with one in front of another (rows). The players raise their arms and space themselves so that fingertips reach fingertips.

Then a right quarter turn is called, and the fingertip test is done again. A call of "streets" means that the players should make a right quarter turn; a call of "alleys" means a left quarter turn. The players' arms are raised so that the runner and "it" have freeways and barricades as a tag is attempted. "It" may not reach across any barricade to tag the runner. The signal caller may effect a change any time he or she chooses.

RELEASE OF TENSION
AND
EXCESSIVE ENERGY
4

Children build up tensions just as adults do, but they tend to reduce them naturally through movement and play. Frequently children are required to be still beyond their capacity to endure. When this happens both tension and excess energy increase, leading to restlessness and lack of attention, which may lead to unnecessary strain between adult and child.

It is more effective to deal directly with the cause (the need to move) than the ensuing behavior. If you can involve children in brief, but enjoyable activities that allow them to wiggle, jiggle, stretch, and/or move with vigor, you may find everyone in a more pleasant mood, including yourself.

For additional information on choosing activities to meet this need, see the Index.

JELLO JIGGLE

Ask the children: "Have you ever seen a bowl of jello jiggle? Have you ever opened the refrigerator and seen it wiggle? It doesn't move like anything else in the whole world. Jam doesn't move that way, and worms don't wiggle that way. It is very special.

"Can you move like jello? Can you let your shoulders jiggle like jello? Try it. Can you let your arms loose to shake like jello? While you are jiggling your arms and shoulders, can you start your hips moving? Can you be loose in the knees? Is your head easy and floppy? Can you wobble very, very slowly until you are in slow motion? A *big, slow* motion wobble. Is your whole body in motion? Can you wobble forward and backward? Can you wobble in a circular fashion? Can you wobble the other direction in a circular motion? Can your wobble include some up and down motions? Do you *feel* loose? Can you wiggle with a friend? Perhaps we could make up a new dance and call it the 'Jello Jiggle'? Do you think we could put it to music?"

Perceptual motor development body awareness; body image; coordination and control

Attention span and concentration fun; flowing; challenging; personally involving

Listening skills series of verbal questions; prolonged listening

Release of tension and excessive energy wiggling out tense spots (as racers shake their arms and hands before a race)

Self-control moving and coordinating all parts of one's body

Development of thinking processes consciously controlling one isolated body part in a specific way; translating problems into solutions

Physical abilities improved physical control

COMMENTS AND SUGGESTIONS

It seems that when tension and stress are reduced, self-control increases or becomes easier.
If you have the gift of storytelling, make up your own story, or perhaps let the children try.
It would be interesting to know if "Can You?" questioning and involvement improves children's general attention span and concentration and promotes better listening skills.
It might be fun to make jello in conjunction with this activity.
Pace is an important aspect of exploring movement. Pause, to allow the children to try each motion.
Remember there are no right and wrong answers in this type of activity. The attempt is the important aspect.

MODIFICATIONS

If the children seem hesitant, shy, or distracted by others you might consider having them do this activity with their eyes closed.
You might combine "Mirroring" and "Jello Jiggle" in slow motion.

I AM A BALLOON

Ask that all children shake loose and collapse as much as possible. Say: "You are a great saggy balloon and you have no air in you. Can you go absolutely limp? Now when you hear this sound, 'shhhh,' you will know that you are being slowly filled with air. Some will fill all over while others may fill only one arm or leg at a time. Let's try it. Shhhh ... sh ... sh ... sh ... shhhhhh." Take your time and allow the children really to work at becoming slowly filled with air. Then say: "Now you are getting just about as full as you can. Shhhhh. ... Are your lungs filled? Are you as big as you can possibly be? Oh! you have developed a *slow* leak, ssss ... Are you beginning to droop? ssssssssssss ... sssssss ... sss ... Are you just about collapsed? Do you feel yourself *totally* collapsed and limp? Is your head heavy? Are your arms and legs completely relaxed? Is your body sinking into the floor (or your chair)? Hey, they put a patch on you. Now they're going to put air in you again." Continue from there.

Perceptual motor development body awareness; body image; body control

Attention span and concentration brief, fun, and involving; fantasizing

Listening skills bases of action and involvement; anticipation

Release of tension and excessive energy deep breathing; stretching in many body areas; relaxing

Self-control controlling the body (swelling to a sense of fullness and then collapsing); changing moods (fantasizing); following directions

Development of thinking processes fantasizing, personifying, translating; thinking about balloons; learning the extent of one's body

Reinforcement of learned information could relate to the study of air

Social growth working alone and independently; not bothering another; being responsible not to bump into each other

Physical abilities body control

COMMENTS AND SUGGESTIONS

Having a balloon on hand might be fun.

This activity can be done sitting or standing.

You might walk around and lift an arm here or there to see if a child can really go limp. Some cannot and need to participate in other activities that can help them learn to relax (see "Jello Jiggle," "Zzzzz," and "Relaxing").

The story of *The Red Balloon* could be used in conjunction with this activity. Also RCA Records has an excellent children's series, "Dance-A-Story," one of which is called "Balloons."

This activity could be used while the children are learning about the elements. You could also include "Paper Plate Play."

This activity could be done in a hospital.

This activity has been used to calm excited children and relax tense, nervous ones.

MODIFICATIONS

If there is plenty of room, blow up a balloon and let it go. It will shoot all over the room, and the children can simulate this action. You might want to be sure they are aware of their "no bumping" responsiblity. ("Cross Over" might be a good preliminary activity.)

You can also have the children be small balloons that get popped by a pin. Here they can learn to collapse and relax quickly but *gently.*

You could tell a story about a weather balloon . . . caught in gusts of wind . . . hit by rain drops . . . floating gently in the sunshine. . . .

OH, MACDONALD

The song, "Oh, MacDonald Had a Farm," becomes a stretching song: "Oh, MacDonald had a body, E–I–E–I–O. And on this body he had an arm, E–I–E–I–O. With a stretch, stretch here, and a stretch, stretch there, and here a stretch, there a stretch, everywhere a stretch, stretch, oh, MacDonald had a body, E–I–E–I–O," etc. Arms, legs, neck, tongue, trunk, toes, etc. can be stretched.

Perceptual motor development body awareness; body image

Attention span and concentration music; changes; active involvement; opportunity to contribute; working in unison

Listening skills listening for clues

Release of tension and excessive energy stretching; change of pace

Self-control opportunity for movement to reduce restlessness

Social growth working in unison with a group; not stretching into another's space (personal space); sense of belonging

Physical fitness increased range of motion from stretching and rotating joints

COMMENTS AND SUGGESTIONS

Body parts can also be rotated.
This activity can be done sitting or standing.

After the children understand the basic pattern, they can select the body parts to be stretched.

This activity could be used with the child(ren) who is learning to identify body parts.

A friend uses this activity as she moves a profoundly retarded child through her stretching movements for the day. She sings the song· very slowly, rubbing the body part as the names it and before stretching it. The child seems to enjoy the combination of song, contact, and movement and may relate to the world a little more for it. (Thanks to Sandy Ackler for this idea.)

This activity could be used in a hospital.

Remember, restless children are trying to *limit* their movement. They need an exercise such as this one, periodically, to express their need to move.

MODIFICATIONS

Children could add a clockwise, then counterclockwise, neck rotation during the words "Oh, MacDonald had a body (clockwise), E–I–E–I–O" (counterclockwise); or if they were standing they could add a clockwise and counterclockwise hip rotation.

LION HUNT

The leader tells an action story in which each line is repeated by the children. For example:

> *Words:* "Let's go on a lion hunt!" (Children repeat.) "Ready? Let's go!" (Children repeat.)

Action: Slapping alternate thighs with hands. (This action continues throughout the entire story except when other movements are used.)

The story can contain all kinds of possibilities:
- swimming a river
- sloshing through a swamp
- sneaking quietly past a sleeping rhino, snake, or some other animal
- climbing a tree
- wiping one's forehead
- being chased by ——— (rapid reversal of all previously taken actions)

Each new part of the story should have an appropriate and enjoyable action.

Attention span and concentration fantasizing; working in unison; perhaps contributing

Listening skills excitement; anticipation; dramatization; chorus-like response

Release of tension and excessive energy change of pace; built-up excitement and suspense, especially final part, which reverses all actions previously taken (based upon a chase); similar to a roller coaster—slow-paced beginning, anticipation, suspense, and final thrill (which leaves the child with a positive sense of relief and freedom)

Self-control working in unison while having fun; mood changes; release from stress; dealing with fear in a safe, creative way

Development of thinking processes fantasizing; creating stories; memory (reversing story sequence) under stress

Social growth being part of a functioning whole; opportunity to contribute; having fun with others

COMMENTS AND SUGGESTIONS

This activity can be done sitting or standing.

After the children are familiar with the basic form, you might like to let them create new stories and actions.

If your group especially enjoys this activity, it might be effectively used for a change of pace. It can be however long or short you wish to make it. You might even challenge the children to create a story that brings them back, ready to eat lunch, by 12:30 sharp. When you first try this activity, be careful not to allow too much time.

This activity could be used with children who have limited movement, e.g., those with cerebral palsy.

MODIFICATIONS

Make up different stories and actions.

If the children have visited a zoo, amusement park, museum, etc., an action story might be a good way to review what they have seen.

BACK TO BACK
and
BUSY BEE

All the children pair up quickly, standing back to back with elbows linked. On the call, "busy bee," all players dash to find a new partner and link elbows again, trying not to be last.

Perceptual motor development body awareness; body image; spatial awareness (estimation and relationships)

Attention span and concentration excitement; fast action; frequent changes; necessity for alertness; challenge; simple decision making; social interaction

Listening skills listening carefully for next challenge; dealing with high noise level, own emotional level, rapid changes, and active physical involvement

Release of tension and excessive energy fast and vigorous action; high stimulation level

Self-control requires body control with high level of excitement; practice in functioning effectively under difficult circumstances

Development of thinking processes multiple, simple decision making; ability to change mind quickly

Social growth much social interaction (because of rapid changes of partners and back-to-back position, players are less apt to seek out their friends—which means the shy or less popular child is not as apt to be left out or chosen last)

Physical abilities agility; body control

Physical fitness perhaps some stretching of chest muscles

COMMENTS AND SUGGESTIONS

This activity reduces the chances of "not being chosen." We need to be sensitive to the effect that various aspects of games and activities can have on children and make selections and modifications accordingly.

If the group is uneven in number, ask a child to give the calls and then immediately try to find a partner.

It is wiser not to emphasize who is last. It isn't usually necessary and can be embarrassing to some children. The attempt and participation are where learning occurs.

This is usually a good time to observe. What is the social interaction of your group? Does any child have difficulty with this activity? Why? etc.

MODIFICATIONS

"Busy Bee": The leader makes calls like "knee to knee," "back to back," "right palm to right palm," "left ear to right knee," etc., while the partners try to follow the calls as quickly as they can. At the call "Busy Bee" everyone changes partners, and the calls begin again. "Back to Back" might be a good preliminary to "Busy Bee."

Develop the degree of simplicity or complexity in this activity according to your group.

CROSSED WIRES

All children hold their noses with one hand while they reach across their bodies to take the opposite ear with the other hand. At a signal, they are to try to uncross their arms and reverse positions.

Perceptual motor development body awareness; body image (parts and positioning); laterality; ability to make moving adjustments (coordination); motor planning

Attention span and concentration basis of activity, but only briefly

Release of tension and excessive energy focuses all attention; brief; change of pace; lowers level of excitement; laughter

Self-control physical and emotional control; problem solving (have a plan and tackle one problem at a time)

Development of thinking processes problem solving; learning to think under stress

Reinforcement of learned information techniques of problem solving (discussed by teacher or learned from experience and personal observation)

Social growth sharing ideas

Physical abilities coordination under stress

COMMENTS AND SUGGESTIONS

You might like to collect these quick challenges to coordination. They are fun and can be used in many creative ways (on auto trips, with neighborhood children, waiting in line, etc.).

The children could suggest ways to help each other, so they all can do the activity. Having the children help each other encourages them to learn about motor planning, expressing an idea, and sharing.

One important idea that usually comes out with time is to move one hand first and then the other, or "solve one problem at a time."

Movement activities help reduce built-up tensions by involving participants so completely in play that they forget about the stressful factors. Movement also brings relief from muscular tension by stretching the tense areas and restoring circulation. An activity such as this or "Pass the Shoe" might be a good way to initiate a problem-solving session.

MODIFICATIONS

Rubbing one's belly while patting one's head (and the reverse) is an old, continuous action version of this type of activity.

Highly skilled players can do three different motions all at once. Children may come up with excellent suggestions.

TEAM JUGGLE

The leader throws an object to a player. That person throws it to another, and so on, until everyone has received the object. Each player must remember to throw always to the *same* person. Now the leader starts the object again, but this time (after waiting a few seconds) starts another object, then another, and so forth. See how many objects the team can juggle at once (see following suggestions on what to stress).

Perceptual motor development visual tracking; spatial awareness (estimation); manipulation of objects; body and space relationships; visual figure and ground; perceiving accurately under stress

Attention span and concentration practice in maintaining attention and concentration through massive extraneous stimuli, high level of excitement, and two-part role playing

Release of tension and excessive energy excitement; intense involvement; focusing attention; some success; acceptable to miss; some laughter (although tension level frequently quite high)

Self-control practice under stress; immediate feedback

Development of thinking processes two-part role playing (attention must be directed to receiving an object, then shifted to passing, and then immediately back to receiving); weeding out irrelevant input

Social growth teamwork; cooperation; consideration of others

Physical abilities eye, hand, object coordination; practice in throwing and catching (follow-through and absorption of force); ability to function physically under stress

COMMENTS AND SUGGESTIONS

Yarn balls, paper wad balls, sock balls, etc. are good to use since they are soft, safe, and not apt to cause damage if missed (see "Making Equipment at Little or No Cost," p. 201).
To make this activity go smoothly and be as beneficial as possible, emphasize each of the following:

- follow through directly at the target
- help the receiver make a successful catch
- have the receiver's attention *before* throwing
- be ready to receive; as soon as you have made a throw return your attention to the player who throws to you

- "absorb" the ball (catch and bring it into your body) so it won't bounce away
- cooperation and team challenge are most significant

You may want to see if you can improve the team record from trial to trial.
This activity could be used in a hospital.

MODIFICATIONS

Increase the number of objects (as a team challenge).
Vary sizes, weights, and texture of objects.

FRANTIC BALL

All players start with a ball on the floor in front of them. The object of the activity is to keep all the balls rolling. If a ball stops and is spotted an official screams and a point is lost. When five points are lost, a time period is over. (The length of time the group continues without losing five points can be timed.) All stopped balls must be put into motion again and are a continuing part of the play. If a ball gets lodged under something accidentally, it is put back into play by an official. If a player deliberately lodges or attempts to hide a ball, and is caught doing so, a point is lost and the ball is put into play again.

Perceptual motor development body control; eye, foot, and object coordination; spatial awareness (estimation and relationships); body and space relationships; balance; visual tracking;

visual figure and ground; temporal awareness (judging rolling speed of ball)

Attention span and concentration refocusing quickly after each action; immediate feedback of effects of focusing and not focusing attention

Release of tension and excessive energy massive bombardment; total involvement; focusing of attention

Self-control determining and planning action

Development of thinking processes trying new ways to tackle problems

Social growth sense of team (without defined roles or positions) and belonging; depending on others to help resolve inordinate number of problems; receives neither praise nor blame for part played on team

Physical abilities thinking and moving quickly; agility; body control; eye, foot, and object control

COMMENTS AND SUGGESTIONS

Thanks to Karl Rohnke of Project Adventure and author of *Cowstails and Cobras* for introducing me to this terrific game.

Since you will need a ball for each player, plus possibly some extras, you might call your tennis-playing friends or local tennis club for old tennis balls. If you have a local tennis ball factory or sporting firm, seek a donation of rejects (Frantic balls do not have to bounce or be "alive").

Other types of balls can be used. Perhaps a variety of sizes, colors, etc. may give the children broader perceptual motor experiences.

You may need volunteers to help officiate. Sometimes children who have temporary health limitations can be asked to help.

Noisemakers to replace a scream can be fun if handy, but sometimes a good scream lets off steam.

Keeping time and score may or may not be necessary depending upon your participants and several other factors. Children may wish to know if they improved their previous attempt but probably only after having played the game several times.

Sometimes children will begin by trying to keep "their" ball rolling. This usually continues for only a short time, but if it persists, use the first modification listed.

Encourage children to use both feet.

Because some of the needs of this game can be met only with experience (effective individual planning, group strategy, etc.) you might want to plan this activity into your program several times over an extended period of time.

Loss of equipment is frequently a problem in all play, but having sufficient balls for "Frantic Ball" is vital. At the end of the game, pick up any extra balls and put them in the bag or box first. Then ask each child to find one ball. If everyone does not have a ball, ask *all* children to help find these balls. Then have each child toss his or her ball into the bag. It seems too simple, but it really works.

MODIFICATIONS

Add an extra ball every fifteen seconds or so, if you feel it would help the activity.

Reduce the number of balls if you think it is necessary.

Have the children use only the left or right foot, or the "other" foot (the one not usually used). This modification can be given to the children as a challenge and does not have to be monitored, but it might be helpful to reduce the number of balls.

A newspaper swatter (see "Comments and Suggestions") is placed on some support, such as a wastepaper basket, in the center of a circle of players. A player is selected to be the first swatter. This player goes to the center, picks up the newspaper, hurries to another player, swats that player below the waist, rushes to replace the swatter across the wastepaper basket, and runs to his or her original place. If the newspaper falls off or into the basket, the original swatter must return and place it across the basket again. The player swatted may grab the newspaper as soon as it is placed across the basket and attempt to swat the one who just swatted him or her. If the player succeeds, the original swatter tries again, swatting another player. If the one swatted cannot swat the swatter in time, then this player becomes the new swatter.

Releasing tension and excessive energy known as a softwar activity; involves aggression without injury; laughing, friendly display of aggression but can also be relatively hostile without harm; active involvement

Physical abilities alertness; reduced reaction time; reduced movement time; agility

COMMENTS AND SUGGESTIONS

A newspaper should be loosely rolled longways so that it will hold up but not be heavy enough to hurt when used as a swatter. You may want an extra newspaper swatter on hand in case the original one becomes limp or badly torn.

If you notice that some children are not getting a turn, have each swatter sit down after swatting. Only those standing can be swatted.

MODIFICATIONS

If you or the children are learning names, have the swatter call the player's name while swatting.

Offer a challenge to those who rarely get caught when they swat: If they are willing they should try to call the name of the player they are going to swat as they remove the newspaper from the wastepaper can.

BEACHBALL VOLLEYBALL

"Beachball Volleyball" can be played with as many or as few rules as you choose. Begin with simple rules and see what your group needs (see "Modifications"). The serve can be a simple punch or throw into the air, and assistance can be given by teammates.

Perceptual motor development visual tracking; body and space relationships; spatial awareness (estimation and relationships); timing; visual figure and ground

Attention span and concentration novelty; involvement; minimal skill requirements (inattention may be caused by lack of chance to participate, and modification could be introduced)

Release of tension and excessive energy involvement; success; moving; stretching; contributing

Self-control playing particular area only (important aspect of team play is sharing with others and learning not to take a play away from another)

Social growth teamwork; consideration of others; sharing; fairness

Physical abilities eye, hand, object coordination; basic skills of volleyball

COMMENTS AND SUGGESTIONS

Because of wind and time required to chase the ball, this game might be better played indoors.

It could be played in limited space, but you would need to put away things that could be knocked over and broken.

Free beachballs can be obtained from companies that use them as advertising gimmicks, or you should be able to purchase one for less than a dollar.

A balloon can be used, but it does not have quite the same flavor. If you use a balloon you might want to put a little water or a few beans in it to give it some weight, which will also make it move erratically.

A piece of colored yarn can act as a net. You can hang additional yarn pieces from it to make it more netlike.

The game can be played standing or sitting (see "In-seat Beachball Volleyball").

You may wish to discuss court coverage and the fun of everyone hitting the ball (see also the final modification listed).

MODIFICATIONS

The game can be played with no rules; simply ask the whole group to hit the ball back and forth over the net as many times as possible (called "Infinity Volleyball"). Allow as many hits to a side as needed; individuals can hit the ball as many times as they need to; no boundaries are used (can play it off the wall); etc.

"In-seat Beachball Volleyball": Players sit in seats so that no light can be seen between the chair seat and the body. (One group nicknamed this game "Buns in Seat" volleyball, its official call when someone forgot and left his or her chair.

If you have a skillful group that plays soccer, they may want to play using any part of the body (head, knee, shoulder, etc.) except hands.

Have a rule in which a player must step out of bounds after hitting the ball three times (honor system). This rule will reduce players on the court to only those who have not hit it as frequently. Allow the ball to be played by those on the sidelines whenever it goes out of bounds. When down to the last person, everyone returns to the court and the game starts all over again.

SELF-CONTROL

5

Self-control seems to be developmental in nature. Some adults hope to be able to reduce a child's disruptive and interferring behavior and elicit some degree of emotional control, whereas others hope to increase a child's independence, self-direction, and effective behavior. Both of these are important and are different degrees of the same need. The possibility of helping any given child is based on that particular child and the time and resources available. Play is such a resource.

Some of the types of play that seem to contribute to and encourage the development of self-control are those that

- allow a child to establish a personal, positive identity as an important member of the group
- encourage social growth and responsibility
- release energy and reduce built-up tensions
- increase attention span and concentration
- promote listening skills
- allow practice in being in control
- involve directing and controlling oneself independently
- require following directions to be successful
- practice changing emotional levels within an activity
- practice functioning (effectively) under stress
- encourage a child to perservere and deal with frustration

Play has some general characteristics that make it a powerful tool in helping a child gain self-control:

- The opportunities to experiment and experience are abundant and continuous.

- Goals and purposes are relatively clear and consistent.
- Self-control frequently contributes to achieving the goal.
- Feedback is usually immediate and frequent, allowing a child to experience relationships between causes and effects.
- There are many possibilities of success and opportunities to see success as available through self-control.
- Errors can be forgiven.
- There is usually an almost instant opportunity to try again (to adjust, to repeat, to recover).
- Progressive challenges can be built in so that a child can succeed at many levels and still see additional possibilities.

For additional related activities, see the Index.

The children pretend to be asleep. You could move among them and test how relaxed they really are (see first modification under "Relaxing"). At the sound of an alarm they jump up and move quickly to another place, where they pretend to fall asleep again. (You might again test their relaxation.)

Release of tension and excessive energy sudden explosive response; practice of two extremes

Self-control changing levels of excitement and tension

Physical abilities ability to relax, move smoothly, and in coordinated manner

COMMENTS AND SUGGESTIONS

The ability to relax quickly and for whatever time is available is a valuable skill and should be developed if at all possible. Residual stress and tension can drain off energy and increase the sense of fatique.

MODIFICATIONS

"Tense & Relax": While the children lie on the floor or sit in a chair, ask them to tense a particular body part (fist, face, shoulders, etc.) and then stretch out the tension, trying to feel the difference between the two.

RELAXING

Children learn to relax and be in control of their body tensions by participating in activities that make them aware of these factors. Being a wind-up toy that gradually runs down, an ice cube or chocolate melting, a puppet, Raggedy Ann and Andy, a tire going slowly flat, or allowing various body parts to swing free and then collapse could be used.

Perceptual motor development isolating body parts (maturation does not guarantee this ability; children may need additional experience); becoming more aware of one's physical state

Attention span and concentration dramatization maintains interest

Release of tension and excessive energy ability to relax learned

Self-control increased neuromuscular relaxation (control of physical reactions to stress)

Development of thinking processes mind-body interaction; conscious control over muscular tension and relaxation

Physical abilities control over isolated body segments

COMMENTS AND SUGGESTIONS

Try to allow time for total relaxation. It will take some children longer than others, but these are probably the children who need this experience most.

If you are a storyteller use your ability to lengthen the time span of this type of activity.

Music sometimes helps.

In a stress-producing world it has become important that children learn to relax as young as possible. Tension and its detrimental effects are being found in increasing numbers of children.

MODIFICATIONS

Have children lie on the floor or sit in chairs with their eyes closed. After they have gradually relaxed, move among them lifting an arm or gently moving a head to determine if they are really totally relaxed. If they resist or assist, try to help them relax further. Children can eventually do this with each other.

(See also "Zzzzz.")

OLD WITCHY-TOE TAG

One player is Old Witchy-Toe, who pretends to be looking for something.

THE PLAYERS CHANT	Old Witchy-Toe, what are you looking for?
WITCHY-TOE	A needle.
GROUP	What do you need a needle for?
WITCHY-TOE	To mend my sack.
GROUP	What do you want a sack for?
WITCHY-TOE	To put YOU in!

At this statement all the group members scatter while Old Witchy-Toe tries to catch someone; that child becomes Old Witchy-Toe, and the chant begins again.

Perceptual motor development body awareness and control; spatial awareness; estimation of distance and speed

Attention span and concentration excitement; control (see "Comments and Suggestions")

Release of tension and excessive energy excitement building to a peak and then exploding

Self-control seemingly wild behavior allowed but also responsibility for not bumping others: playing with edge of control (also good way to experience coping with fear)

Development of thinking processes taking risks at personal level; thinking and responding effectively when excited; adequately monitoring situations

Social growth responsibility for others

Physical abilities body control; agility; rapid starting and stopping

COMMENTS AND SUGGESTIONS

Thanks to Michele Budich for teaching me this game.
Being careful not to run into someone else should be stressed, unless the children are already capable. "Cross Over" might be a good preliminary game to help the children avoid bumping into each other.
Young children seem to enjoy the repetition and stimulation of this game. It may be that they enjoy being excited and afraid when the timing and outcome are in their control. Each child may be as near or as far from Old Witchy-Toe at the end of the

chant as he or she chooses. Thus they can individually determine how ready they are to take a chance and how much of a risk they are willing to take.

SAFE FROM THE SHARKS

Children are divided into groups of three. (Use extras or one group of three as sharks.) Two players from each group form a "safe" underwater cage by facing each other and joining hands. The third player is the diver who wishes to avoid the sharks. The diver stands inside the cage. When the leader calls "change cages," the cage players raise their hands and all divers try to scurry for another cage. A shark can tag any diver not in a cage. A tagged diver changes places with the tagger. The game should be divided into approximately three equal time periods, allowing each member of the group a chance to be a diver or shark.

Perceptual motor development body control; spatial awareness; timing; adaptability and adjustment

Attention span and concentration exciting; taking risks

Listening skills verbal signal

Release of tension and excessive energy excitement; movement; risks

Self-control problem solving under stress

Development of thinking processes decision making; problem solving with rapid adapting; strategy

Social growth cooperation; responsibility to avoid bumping into others; dealing with situation in which someone else is moving toward same space

Physical abilities agility; dodging

COMMENTS AND SUGGESTIONS

A random or circle formation might be used for this activity.
Allow only one diver to a cage.
Those who are sharks at the end of a time period can also begin the next time period as sharks.
A tag below the waist may be safer and less apt to cause a fall.
Squirrel in the Tree is a simplified version of this activity. If your group cannot handle the stimulation of the idea of sharks or the excitement of tagging, you might consider this version, or you could create your own.

MODIFICATIONS

Always feel free to add ground rules or modifications to help the game as played by your particular group.
A game can be made more or less exciting depending on the scene that is set. Sharks are exciting, Martians maybe a little less exciting, zoo keepers even less. Meet the needs of your group.
Have only one shark.
Instead of divers there could be two or three types of fish (e.g., red snapper, goldfish, blue fish). The cages could be rocks safe for hiding. When one fish is called, only these particular players change rocks while the shark (might be best to reduce to one) tries to catch one of them. A call of "all fish swim" would mean that all fish find a new rock.

PASS THE SHOE

All players sit in a circle with some object to pass in front of them. They can select objects from among their things or you can supply them. On the beat, each child places the object in front of the player on his or her right. This rhythm pattern continues until the word "do," at which point the players do not leave the "shoe" in front of the receiver but rather bring it back in front of themselves. On the words "I do!" the object is again placed in front of the receiver and left there. The pattern is repeated.

Perceptual motor development timing (temporal awareness); eye, hand, object coordination; perceiving audio clues

Attention span and concentration music; constant involvement; movement; pattern change; responsibility to the group (attention challenged by amount of activity continuously occurring)

Listening skills passing on the beat; hearing key words

Self-control learning to stay calm

Development of thinking processes solving problems individually and as a group (under stress); learning to anticipate change from clues

Social growth group challenge; individual responsibility

Physical abilities manual dexterity; object manipulation; timing

POSSIBLE PROGRESSION

Have the children learn song (see Figure 5-1). Perhaps clapping on the "passing" beat would help. Passing the objects, the song could be sung slowly with strong emphasis on the passing beat. The group should try for completion without a mishap. (For those groups that may have great difficulty, you might try using only a few objects; those not having an object to pass would slap the floor as if they did have one.)

COMMENTS AND SUGGESTIONS

Sometimes children are embarrassed to pass their "shoe" for one reason or another. Thus it may be better to allow them to choose their objects. Variety in size and shape may increase the perceptual motor challenge.

Mishaps will usually occur and shouldn't be taken too seriously. Discourage the children from blaming each other when objects pile up in front of one child.

It is fun for the children to realize they are improving as a group. You might encourage the group with a challenge to finish a certain number of rounds without a pileup. You might stress the responsibility of the person passing the shoe. A pass can help or hinder the process.

As group size increases so does the possibility of mishaps. If you have a large group and they are having difficulty, you could divide them into smaller groups. Or you could divide them in half and have one-half watch while the other half plays; then observers could make suggestions about improving the game.

At first you may want to avoid objects that are very flat or otherwise difficult to pick up. Objects like paper wad balls are good for beginners.

This activity can lead to a discussion of how to solve problems when they "pile up." If when objects pile up in front of one individual that player remains calm and continues to move just one object at a time—solve one problem at a time—the problem will tend to resolve itself.

MODIFICATIONS

This game can also be played at desks if they are placed in a close circle.

The children can challenge themselves by trying to use their other hand. This can be offered as an individual option so those children who are ready can try it but those who are still having difficulties can concentrate on process and pattern.

Two players sitting across from each other can also play this game, and it may be a good way to begin with some children. They can move to a larger group after they learn the basic pattern. After the group is fairly proficient the tempo can be increased.

YOU MUST PASS THE SHOE FROM ME TO YOU, TO YOU, YOU MUST
PASS THIS SHOE AND DO JUST WHAT I DO!

Figure 5–1

FOX AND SQUIRREL

The children form a circle. Two objects are passed around the circle. One is designated as a squirrel, the other as a fox. The fox can be passed only to the *next* player in the circle, but in either direction. The squirrel can *leap* across the circle and also can go in either direction. The fox tries to catch the squirrel, while the squirrel tries to avoid being caught. Each player must determine his or her response according to the object received. If the squirrel is caught, the game begins again.

Perceptual motor development eye, hand, object coordination (under stress); visual tracking

Attention span and concentration excitement, lots of fast action; no predictable action pattern (suspense) (two or three objects doing different things at once *challenges* ability to concentrate)

Release of tension and excessive energy laughter; total involvement; even confusion

Self-control challenging; alright to try again

Development of thinking processes changing roles and objective at any moment

Physical abilities passing and catching: object manipulation

COMMENTS AND SUGGESTIONS

Try to make the objects to be passed clearly different. Later you may wish to make the distinction more difficult.

To lead up to the activity you might have the children pass the squirrel and then the fox, seeing if the fox can catch the squirrel (both going the same direction and not leaping). After the children have the basic idea, you might add the leap of the squirrel and allow the fox to go in either direction.

This activity is not to be taken too seriously, and really can't be, since players are usually not quite sure who they are for or against.

MODIFICATIONS

A circle can be too large to allow the fox to catch the squirrel. When this occurs the "squirrel" players could risk (and increase the challenge) letting the fox get nearer, leaping only when necessary and taking smaller leaps (teasing the fox); or the children could function as two circles (the players must be familiar with the game). This game can be played at almost any level of sophistication. An activity that can grow and change with the changing abilities of its participants can become developmental in nature, and thus the role of the planner becomes even more important.

If certain rules do not seem to work for your group (e.g., the squirrel can go in both directions), try changing them. No activity is perfectly created for all groups. Try new ways. (You might want to consider one change at a time.)

Add a second fox; This is really wild, fun, and confusing.

VAMPIRE

All players close their eyes. One is designated as a vampire. The players wander around the room. If the vampire touches someone he or she pretends to bite that child (on the shoulder). The bitten player is now also a vampire and seeks other victims. If two vampires bite each other they are neutralized and become regular players—until bitten again; for this reason the game has no end.

Perceptual motor development spatial awareness; kinesthetic awareness

Attention span and concentration scary excitement; closed eyes (but this situation may not induce transfer to less scary ones)

Release of tension and excessive energy cathartic effect

Self-control personal challenges

COMMENTS AND SUGGESTIONS

Use some volunteers to help you prevent players from wandering off or moving toward hazards. This also allows these children to accept responsible roles.

Be aware of obstacles that players may bump into.

In activities where children cannot see and may be afraid, I would recommend that you have them close their eyes rather than using blindfolds. If some children need to peek, let them. Instead of policing, encourage the children to challenge themselves by keeping their eyes closed. The children should learn to direct themselves. We may find that they are their own best progression builders, if given alternatives and growth-producing experiences. Try to be patient.

Be aware that this activity may be very frightening for some children. It may be best to let them stay out the first few times until they are ready to participate. Allowing them to be responsible helpers may give them an opportunity to grow and overcome their fear without embarrassment.

A good preliminary activity might be "Cows and Ducks," which has many of the same elements but is less frightening, or

"Safe from the Sharks," which can be frightening but does not require closed eyes.

A scream can be added, either blood curdling or soft. This choice is best made by you.

MODIFICATIONS

Once bitten, a player joins hands with the original vampire and they become a "team vampire." Thus the game has an end (vampires do not neutralize each other). This version also encourages the strategy of listening for players and seeking safe areas.

A bitten player could "die," drop to the floor, and become an obstacle. If this version is used it might be safer to have all the players crawl on the floor rather than walking around.

STREAMERS

The children merely move a crepe paper streamer around in the air in as many different circular patterns as possible. This is a simple, but creative, piece of play equipment that has been with us, in one form or another, since children first found pleasure in watching a ribbon, scarf, or piece of paper flutter through currents of air.

Perceptual motor development body and space relationships

Attention span and concentration opportunity to create; something to show and share; possible group involvement; moving in unison

Listening skills music could be involved

Release of tension and excessive energy moving; stretching; change of pace; and peaceful fluttering of streamer

Self-control working together in a group

Development of thinking processes creative; memory needed

Social growth belonging and being responsible to a group; following; making contributions; sharing ideas; compromising; leading

Physical fitness developing shoulder girdle: flexibility and range of motion, shoulder alignment, development of upper back muscles, reduction of tension in this area

COMMENTS AND SUGGESTIONS

See "Making Equipment at Little or No Cost," p. 201.
This can develop into a good playground activity, an opportunity for individual, quiet involvement, an opportunity to participate in a demonstration for others, a break on long car trips, a present to make and share with a friend, and/or a replacement for dangerous fireworks on the Fourth of July.
Perhaps your group would like to participate in a local parade or school demonstration. This activity is possible for all skill levels and at the same time helps develop the participant physically, emotionally, and socially.
Fancier streamers can be made by adding a string and the weight of cardboard to the hand end. (Experience makes me question whether these additions increase the fun or other benefits.)
The streamers can be used individually or in large group formations of spontaneous or carefully choreographed patterns. This

exercise can bring about a simple, quiet joy and a sense of overwhelming togetherness.

MODIFICATIONS

The following could be played with streamers:

- Follow Me
- Mirroring
- Can You Do This?
- Detective
- Trying to Remember

A dance could be created using one or two streamers.
Perhaps a creative physical therapist could develop ROM (range of motion) activities for children to do on their own between therapy sessions.

PARTS AND POINTS

The leader challenges the children by asking them to place body parts (ear, foot, shoulder, etc.) and points (elbow, nose, knee, etc.) in some position or against some object or other part of their body. Example: "Place one body part against the wall; place another body part above its normal position; touch two points of your body together; touch a third point on the floor; touch one ear with some body part." These actions are done sequentially and are cumulative. All are held for at least five seconds after the last request is completed.

Perceptual motor development instructions could be developed for particular problems

Attention span and concentration brief, progressive challenge

Listening skills hearing instructions of two or more parts

Release of tension and excessive energy twisting and stretching; being challenged; succeeding (or laughing); doing the ridiculous

Self-control activity should be modified to challenge rather than threaten abilities

Development of thinking processes interpretation; motor planning; problem solving; individual decision making

Physical abilities balance

COMMENTS AND SUGGESTIONS

This activity has been used to calm children when they have just come from an experience that encouraged hyperactivity and there was a need to reduce their activity level.
This activity could be used as a quick break.
If you are comfortable with the challenge let the children give you a sequence of five directions and see if you can do it. Children's challenges can be very difficult, and you may not succeed. But if the emphasis has been on the effort rather than on the success or failure, you and the children should be able to be comfortable with failure.
Perhaps a creative physical therapist could develop specific challenges for individual patients.
See "Can You Do This?"
This might be a good time to take pictures.

This game can be played sitting as well as standing.
The challenge could be made easier or harder, longer or shorter.
You could make a spinner wheel (like the game called "Twister")
with various options, or you could draw three-by-five inch cards
from a box.
After you complete the directions, ask the children to close their
eyes and hold their positions for five or more seconds.

RHYTHMS

The players sit in a circle or in a random formation. A rhythm is
established. All the players slap their thighs twice, clap twice,
and snap their fingers on one hand and then the other. Once the
rhythm has been established, a player is chosen to begin. This
player calls his or her own first name on the first snap of the
fingers and any other person's name on the second snap. The
player called then continues the pattern.

Perceptual motor development patterning (recognition and
duplication) (see "Comments and Suggestions")

Attention span and concentration continuous participation
(pace); anticipation (uncertainty); moving in unison

Listening skills hearing names over noise of snapping of
fingers (audio figure and ground)

Release of tension and excessive energy coping with stress

Self-control coping with stress in a safe environment (encourages risk); improvement evident

Development of thinking processes decision making under stress

Social growth teaches patience, acceptance, and support of others (I have seen children share in the joy of a child who is finally able to come in on the first snap; this is very positive social growth)

Physical abilities temporal and physical coordination under stress

COMMENTS AND SUGGESTIONS

With some groups the hand pattern may pose a real challenge by itself and could be tried several different times as a preliminary to the activity.
You may find that creating hand patterns (that the children do as a group) is an activity in its own right.
At first bringing the names in on the right beat may prove difficult for some children, and you may wish to let a player wait (missing a set or two of the sequence) until he or she can come in on the first snap. To have a child fail if he or she is not able to come in on the very next sequence may create too much frustration for learning to occur and may also stop the activity too frequently. You can establish an atmosphere in which it is *really* acceptable not to come in on the very next snap. Children who are learning self-control must have the opportunity to struggle as well as to succeed.
A group challenge might be to see if all members of the group

can be called before anyone is called twice. This is a difficult challenge to the memory and also gets everyone involved.

MODIFICATIONS

Simplify the hand pattern for a group that finds this pattern too complex.

Numbers can be used instead of names.

If your group needs an additional challenge, have them form a circle. Each person is given a number in sequence around the circle. The pattern begins with 1 and is passed in sequence. If a child misses (doesn't come in on the beat), he or she goes to the end of the line and all children after this player move up one place, thereby changing their numbers. If the children can do this, allow the numbers to be called in random order.

REMEMBER, ACTIVITIES ARE MODIFIED FOR A PURPOSE: MEETING THE NEEDS OF YOUR GROUP.

DEVELOPMENT
OF
THINKING PROCESSES
6

In games and activities we have a fertile and largely uncultivated source of stimulation for the growing mental processes. There are activities that have multiple problem-solving and decision-making opportunities, activities in which one must think and function quickly under stress. There are games that are won by strategy, where it is imperative to be able to monitor the situation with a keen eye and ear, where memory is the key and participation encourages its development.

It is time to destroy the myth that the mind disengages as the body engages. Consider how many of these factors of cognition can actively occur and be practiced in play:

- preparedness, alertness
- attending, concentrating
- receiving, perceiving
- pattern recognition, relationships and contrasts
- selectivity, discrimination
- comprehension, translation, interpretation, extrapolation
- analysis
- generating alternative solutions
- synthesis
- decision making
- motor planning
- sequencing
- memory, storage
- translating from one mode to another
- appropriate application of information
- transfer of learning
- evaluation

Several people who have worked extensively with children have stressed the relationship between moving and thinking in the developing child.

> The early motor or muscular responses of the child, which are the earliest behavioral responses of the human organism, represent the beginnings of a long process of development and learning. Through these first motor explorations, the child begins to find out about himself and the world around him, and his motor experimentation and his motor learnings become the foundation upon which such knowledge is built. In early childhood, mental and physical activities are closely related,[1] and motor activities play a major role in intellectual development. To a large extent, so-called higher forms of behavior develop out of and have their roots in motor learning.[2]

Perhaps it is time for us to *select* play experiences based on their positive contribution to mental development. Not all activity reinforces or encourages the same thinking processes. Activities may involve a particular cognitive ability at a particular developmental level. Selection and modification become important to utilize play most effectively as a resource for the development and practice of thinking processes. It is exciting to realize that something which holds so much pleasure (play) can also hold so much potential in relation to this serious area.

See the Index for additional related information.

---

[1] Arthur Jersild, *Child Psychology* (Englewood Cliffs, N.J.: Prentice-Hall, Inc., 1954).

[2] Newell C. Kephart, *The Slow Learner In the Classroom* (Columbus, Ohio: Charles E. Merrill Books, Inc., 1960), p. 35.

Have children dramatize all forms of weather by walking as if they are feeling it.

Attention span, concentration, and listening skills individual interpretation; level of participation determined by care in listening

Release of tension and excessive energy and self-control change of routine; role playing; freedom to express oneself; reduction in group conformity

Development of thinking processes imagination; creativity; decision making

Reinforcement of learned information could be part of study of weather and environmental awareness

Physical abilities using the body as a means of expression

COMMENTS AND SUGGESTIONS

Possible weather conditions are:

windy	fall, walking in leaves
sunny	hurricane
pleasant	tornado
very hot	lightening storm
very cold	drizzle
icy	very still (perhaps a good final
muddy	activity for relaxing and
puddles after a rain	quieting the children)

If you are a good storyteller, weave a story around the weather.

Stories can become more involving when a child can imagine the feeling of a particular weather condition. Weather is frequently used to set a mood in a story.

MODIFICATIONS

Have the children walk as if they are in various substances or places:

in deep snow	eggs
in oil or marbles	around a sleeping tiger
in quick sand or tar	on the moon
in molasses or glue	on a tight rope
on worms	on hot coals or hot sand

Have the children walk as if they were in certain places:

into a salad bowl	off a cliff
through a toy shop	at a circus
through a jar of jam	through a dream
in a jungle	in a haunted house
in a zoo	inside a drain to the sewer to a
in a park	treatment plant and back
in busy traffic	through the faucet
in a house with a million friendly cats	

The children could do "mood" walks (sad, happy, tired, worried, etc.).
They could walk like a bear, an old person, a centipede, a baby just learning to walk, a toad or a kangaroo, an inch worm . . . .
Ask the children for other possibilities, and let yourself be creative.

PAPER PLATE PLAY

The object of this activity is to move around in the available space while carrying a paper plate on one's body (balanced or held on by air flow) and avoiding any other object or individual.

Perceptual motor development spatial awareness and body image (and their relationship to each other); body control

Attention span and concentration focusing on problem; watching others (object-centered problem allows shy or uncomfortable children to focus on the object and/or solutions rather than themselves)

Release of tension and excessive energy control of energy level; stretching

Self-control choices and personal alternatives; own pace

Development of thinking processes exploration of alternatives; understanding by doing; making choices

Reinforcement of learned information understanding air flow

Social growth being aware of others; sharing space; assuming responsibility to avoid collisions

Physical abilities balance; body control and coordination

Physical fitness stretching; range of motion and joint involvement

Thanks to Phil Gerney of Cheltenham, Pennsylvania, for introducing me to this activity.
If there is only a limited amount of space available you may want to:

- emphasize balancing the plate and moving in slow motion
- have only part of the group active at one time
- try the respiratory exercise (see "Modifications").

You could relate the original version to the study of air flow (why a kite or airplane stays up). Perhaps making and flying paper airplanes would be an interesting combination with this activity.

MODIFICATIONS

Sheets of newspaper or any piece of paper could be used.
The children could play "Cross Over" and/or "Carpet Skiing" before this activity so that they have developed the ability to avoid bumping into each other.
Balancing the paper plate by one child could be combined with another child trying to blow it away (respiratory exercise). Moving, but no touching, is allowed.

PARTNER TAG

Partners hook one elbow and also form an outside "hook" with the other elbow by placing fist on hip. Two players are free to run. One is designated as "it," and the other tries to avoid being tagged. The chased player may gain safety by hooking on to any of the free elbow hooks. When this occurs the partner of the player who has been hooked onto is no longer safe and can be tagged. If tagged, that player becomes "it" and chases the unhooked player.

Attention span and concentration fast action; unpredictable; involving

Release of tension and excessive energy concentration; involvement; excitement; laughter

Self-control dealing with a given situation effectively (player must be alert, thinking, and able to function under positive stress)

Development of thinking processes watching and then actively participating requires mental alertness

Social growth socially oriented; social in nature

Physical abilities fast reaction time; agility

COMMENTS AND SUGGESTIONS

Because of the complexity and exciting nature of this activity you might want to have a few demonstration trials in slow motion.

If the groups are uneven one group could be a threesome, or you could play (if you were being chased you could hook on; if you were "it" and unable to catch someone, you could either use strategy or ask for a helper to take your place). Children do enjoy having you play with them.

There may be confusion about who is "it." It sometimes helps if a soft object, such as a yarn ball or hat, is carried by the tagger and used for tagging (also safer).

You could also encourage the children to help each other figure out who is "it" if confusion occurs. Frequently this type of problem may be ended quicker by letting the players solve it.

If there is a question about whether a person was tagged before hooking, *you* should make a quick decision (it does not always have to be right), simply announcing who is "it" and perhaps who is being chased.

If you have a group that is uncomfortable hooking elbows, you could have an option of side of foot to side of foot for those who do not want to hook elbows. Usually during the excitement of the game elbows eventually become hooked.

MODIFICATIONS

If your group plays this game well, you could make it more difficult by allowing either "it" or the chased player to hook on. Then all players must keep track of who is "it" and who is being chased.

TASTES AND SMELLS

Have the children taste or smell something. Then ask them to guess what it is. Ask them to *describe* it. Encourage them to think about how these things could also be *assigned feelings* or moods (a difficult assignment). Then ask them to *try* to *express* these *feelings in movement.*

Development of thinking processes practicing smell and taste input; relating knowing to feeling.

Reinforcement of learned information could be related to a sensory unit in science

COMMENTS AND SUGGESTIONS

Some suggestions of things that smell and/or taste are

chocolate	perfume
aftershave lotion	something burnt
freshly cut grass	ammonia
cookie	earth
your ideas	salt
lemon slices	grape
popped popcorn	

If you have no props, ask the children to use their imaginations. Encourage them to *investigate* how the taste or smell makes them feel. Encourage uniqueness and differences; there are no right answers. The pace of this type of activity is vital, and there may be points at which the children will need time really to contemplate. You play an important role in the development of such activities. Perhaps if we were a bit patient we could allow the children to go beyond the immediate, common, or taught responses.

Perhaps this activity could be incorporated with art or writing, e.g., "How does a lemon taste?" "How does it make me feel?" Try carefully to avoid value judgments—which is difficult. Perhaps you could use statements of fact: "That's how the taste of chocolate makes you feel; "You seem to have some feelings about the smell of ammonia"; "I seem to sense some definite feelings in your movements." Or if you are asked, "Is this O.K.?" or "Do you like this?" You might respond with a question that returns the evaluation to the child, e.g., "How do you feel about it?" "Do you like it?" "Which of your movements do you feel best expresses your feelings?"

Taste and smell are frequently neglected skills that if developed could add pleasure, make an individual more aware of the environment, and on occasion save a life.

MODIFICATIONS

It might be interesting to have the children taste or smell a single object, think about it, and the next day continue with the activity. Contemplation and creativity may require time for some children.

MEMORY TEASER TESTER

Have a small group of children stand up in front of the others. All the children (including those in front of the group) try to remember the order in which the children are standing. These children now change places. After a ten-second count or some vigorous exercise (like running in place or fifteen hops), all players jot down the order in which they believe the group was standing. Then ask a volunteer to put the children in the original order (without looking at notes). If the first volunteer cannot do it correctly, allow someone else or the whole group to help.

Perceptual motor development visual sequencing and discrimination; awareness of relationships and patterns

Attention span and concentration objective emphasizes attention and concentration: modifications prevent children from becoming bored if the task seems simple or threatened, if too difficult (see first modification)

Development of thinking processes memory; perceiving patterns and relationships

COMMENTS AND SUGGESTIONS

Place only a few children in the initial line and increase the number as the group progresses.

Ask your group, "How many had the first person in the right place? How many had the first two people in the right order? Three?" Try to encourage them. You might want each child to keep a record to see if there is improvement as time passes. Then you could add another question: "How many of you did as well or better than last time?" Checking for improvement allows the children to feel successful.

The children could share their ideas about what helps them remember.

MODIFICATIONS

To allow some opportunity for success by as many children as possible, you might ask that each volunteer place two players in position. Try to be aware of the child who has difficulty sequencing or remembering, and if that child volunteers let him or her arrange the first two (which are usually easiest to remember).

Have each person in line make a movement (to be remembered). The line stays in this order, but the rest of the group must stand; as each person in line calls his or her name, all other players (including other players in line) try to do the correct action. If you feel some children are following others rather than remembering, ask them all to shut their eyes. Some may still feel the need to peek, but trying to remember will be encouraged. In this modification, the level of difficulty can be varied by having each individual in line repeat the sequence three times.

Be creative; try to develop the potential ability of your group.

Players stand shoulder to shoulder in a line and count off by twos. All number ones turn and face the other direction. The player at one end becomes "it" (the chaser), and the player at the other end must avoid the tag. All the other children must remain in line, but if the chaser tags one of them on the back, he or she becomes "it." Their position in line is then filled by the old chaser.

The tagger needs a great deal of strategy to catch the runner; the runner must remain alert.

Attention span and concentration unpredictable possibility of active participation

Development of thinking processes interpreting action; reacting quickly; using strategy; decision making and problem solving

Social growth seeking help and helping another; developing strategies *together*

Physical abilities thinking and moving (motor planning); agility; being able to stop and start quickly

COMMENTS AND SUGGESTIONS

When children count off for any activity, it may help to have them hold up their fingers to indicate their numbers. In addition to helping those children who tend to forget their numbers, it gives them a technique to help them remember in the future.

Discourage long chases by having a countdown (ten seconds) in which "it" must either tag the chased player or tap a player in line. If the chased player cannot be caught, declare her or him a champion and ask the runner to choose a new runner.

To encourage participation by all, have each child who has been active sit down as he or she re-enters the line. These sitting players cannot be tapped.

In some versions of this game the players in line are squatting. Since there is some question about the potential hazard to the knee joint in a deep knee bend (greater than a forty-five degree angle) with the weight of the body over it, it is important to evaluate this position in various games. In many cases it can be effectively eliminated or replaced. The American Medical Association has discouraged the use of *deep* knee bends, ducks, and squats.

After the children learn this game they may be able to create more than one line, thus having two games going at once and giving the children the opportunity for greater independence and self-control.

MODIFICATIONS

Another version allows the chased player to be the one who can tap a player in line, who then takes his or her place.

After the children are familiar with these simple versions of line tag, they may like to try a more difficult form. This version allows *either* "it" or the runner to tap a player in line to take his or her place. Players in line must be alert to which player is "it and who was tapped.

SHADOWS

Darken the room, and have the children stand between a strong light and a wall. Have them create shadows and shapes so that they can identify their shadows. Children can create shapes alone or with partners. They might like to create a particular shape and have others try to identify it. Stories can be created in shadow plays.

A frightening shadow can be introduced from an overhead projector. A cardboard cutout (such as a witch) or a pencil, moved around on top of the projector, can be something the children can try not to let touch their shadows. Because of the excitement in this type of activity, you may want to slow the pace when you first introduce the frightening objects.

Perceptual motor development body image; body and space relationships; spatial awareness (estimation and relationships); visual directional awareness

Attention span and concentration unique activity holds interest (unless only part of group can participate)

Release of tension and excessive energy usable space and number participating affect how much excess energy (shy children comfortable because focus on shadow, not on them)

Self-control learning to be excited and have fun but not be chaotic (warn children that *they* must control the situation or else less exciting activities will be used; then follow through if necessary, not as a punishment but as part of a learning process)

Development of thinking processes creating; seeing relationships; observing self as a moving entity

Social growth being aware of others, sharing, letting another have space, waiting for turn

Physical abilities practicing dodging

COMMENTS AND SUGGESTIONS

You may want to test this activity before you use it with your group so that you know the requirements; distances, equipment, and so on.

Consider encouraging the children to use their whole bodies to create the shapes.

You may have to pace this activity since children sometimes get very excited.

This is a good activity for Halloween.

Try out some various sized cutouts before use to see which sizes work best.

This activity could be used in hospitals, physical therapy, and recreational therapy by creative leaders.

The children could do this activity at home with their families, where they might also like to try drawing profile silhouettes.

Music might encourage some interesting possibilities.

MODIFICATIONS

You could make a shadow shape and ask the children to reproduce it (like "Follow Me").

You could also hang a sheet between the light and the audience. Each child can be allowed to make his or her favorite shadow, or you can create an activity around these props.

Figure 6–1

LION, HUNTER, GUN

Split group approximately in half. Each team caucuses to determine what its role will be. Possible choices for roles are lion (growling with claws and teeth showing), hunter (standing at attention with a salute), or gun (both hands up like shooting a rifle, plus a loud bang). The teams stand on lines, about twelve inches apart, facing each other. All repeat "lion, hunter, gun, 1, 2, 3" with the leader and then quickly enact their roles. Possible results are:

- lion overpowers hunter
- hunter controls gun
- gun shoots lion

The teams regroup and try again.

Release of tension and excessive energy excitement; explosive nature; running and tagging

Self-control clearly defined times for control and its opposite; waiting has perceived purpose and is limited

Development of thinking processes decision making; strategy; predicting other team's choices; remembering signals; knowing what affects what and how; acting quickly

Social growth group decision making; listening to others; interacting; contributing

COMMENTS AND SUGGESTIONS

This is similar to the game "Rock, Paper, Scissors," with which you may be more familiar (a Chinese version).

The leader's dramatic presentation can set the scene.

This game could be played by children who are not ambulatory. If you use a running version, create safe areas to which children can run.

Adjust the distance to the safety zones and between team lines according to your space and participants.

Avoid using a wall as a safety zone.

POSSIBLE PROGRESSION

Each child selects a role. The leader calls "lion," "hunter," or "gun," and the children who have selected this role respond with appropriate motion and noise.

Two teams face each other. A representative from each team draws a card held by the leader. Each card gives one role. The representatives show the cards to their teams. All say "Lion, Hunter, Gun, 1, 2, 3" and enact their role, later deciding who overcame or conquered whom.

The play is the same as above, but the teams decide what roles they will play.

The teams make a first and second choice each time they caucus. In case of the same call (tie), they can make another attempt without taking time out to meet again.

Tagging without running is added. Both teams should now have sufficient space to step back to avoid being tagged. Taggers can reach but not step. Now those who receive the advantage of the call must also tag their opponent to succeed.

Tagging with running is added, and safety zones are needed.

The team can add those caught or remain the same size (not taking captives).

Note that the chase can be included or eliminated.

CHANGING ENDS (THE UNEVEN BOXES)

An even number of players are placed in an uneven number of spaces, leaving the space in the middle empty. The object is for all players to move in such a way that they end up on the opposite side from which they started. Rules: (1) only one player can move at a time; (2) like checkers, a player can move only one space or jump one other player; and (3) a player can only move in one direction.

Attention span and concentration see the last modification

Self-control learning to work with problem-solving group: to listen to others, test and evaluate ideas, clearly express own suggestions

Development of thinking processes problem solving; recognizing a pattern;

Social growth each group functions differently (a study in group dynamics)

COMMENTS AND SUGGESTIONS

This game has been played with coins or colored discs in boxes on a piece of paper. You might wish to include one variation before, during, or after the moving version, or you may wish to try it out yourself.

Try to indicate the spaces in some easy way. Lines, marks, or flat objects can be used rather than box shapes, which may save time and marking materials.

Perhaps this game could be played when delays occur, e.g.,

waiting for transportation that hasn't yet arrived. This is a good game for a rainy day when everybody has to stay in.

You can split a large group into smaller groups, all working at one time. These groups can vary in size (from four to six). Not all groups can function this independently.

This problem is not always solved quickly or easily, and you will want to plan accordingly. It may help to indicate its level of difficulty and state a time limit (e.g., fifteen minutes) (with an opportunity to try again another time).

Some leaders like to discuss the group's problem-solving with the groups; some prefer to leave any observations to each individual. I believe the modifications encouraging everyone in the group to understand how to solve the problem are good in that they allow all the children to become more involved in the process.

MODIFICATIONS

The more boxes, the more complex the problem seems.

After a group has solved the problem, ask them to do it again. Then have them do it again, but without using any *verbal* communication (perhaps letting other groups watch). Then you might ask the group to do it again, but with no communication of *any* kind (to see if all the players understand the pattern of the solution). Perhaps before this last variation, the group should have some practice on its own.

GOING ON A TRIP

Every child is asked to select some motion or movement he or she would like to share with the group. Ask for volunteers, thus giving some children time to think and providing examples for those who may not have any immediate ideas.

A circle is formed, and the trip begins: "I am Carol and I am going to take this on our trip." The next player says: "Carol is going to take a [motion]. I am Jimmy and I am going on the trip too. I am going to take [motion]." The next player says: "Carol is going to take [motion]; Jimmy will take [motion]; and I am Sue and I am going on our trip too and I am going to take [motion]." And so on.

Perceptual motor development duplication of movement

Attention span and concentration requires continuous attention and concentration (see "leader's challenge" in "Comments and Suggestions"

Listening skills if learning names

Release of tension change of pace

Development of thinking processes memory: audiovisual relationship; relationship between familiar (name and person) and unfamiliar (motion)

Social growth sharing; contributing; leading; following; possibly learning names

COMMENTS AND SUGGESTIONS

This type of activity is helpful when a new child enters the group.

It helps adults learn or review the children's names.

You may want to start with volunteers so that no child has to become tense about not having a motion.

A "leader's challenge" can be added to keep everyone alert. It allows the leader to turn to any player, at any time, and challenge his or her ability to do all or part of the previous names and motions. The entire group could also be challenged.

The children may have to interact with each other to keep track of all the motions and names. This interaction is helpful and should be allowed unless you find it disruptive.

MODIFICATIONS

The children could take an object with them that they must describe by movement.

Encourage the children to take something that rhymes with their names, e.g., Jane–cane, Dawn–fawn, Jim–Tim, Mike–bike. Some names are difficult to rhyme. Help can be soliticted from other children, or that child should be allowed to take a favorite item.

If the activity seems slow, several children could show their movements, and then the entire group could repeat each of these as you place your hand over each child's head. Then several more children could add their movements, and the entire class would try to do the individuals in both of these groups, and so on.

If you have a large group, you might do a few movements each day, repeating some of the ones already done as you move along. You might use this activity daily to reduce restlessness. Doing only a few each day would also give some children an opportunity to think about what they would like to do.

TRYING TO REMEMBER

Select or have the children select movements (such as jumping jacks, sitting down, standing up, running in place, hands overhead as high as possible, head circles, hip rotations) and assign a signal or number to each action. The object is to try to remember what number or signal calls for what movement.

Attention span and concentration *learning* which action goes with which number; *recalling* this information

Release of tension and excessive energy challenge; vigorous activity

Development of thinking processes establishing relationships

Physical fitness good basic exercise (see the introduction to Chapter 9)

COMMENTS AND SUGGESTIONS

Encourage participants to avoid outside clues whenever possible. However, remember that the philosophy of this book is to help children meet their needs. That is, the players are in the respected position of knowing their own needs and being the best judges of their level of challenge. If people are really free to choose, they will challenge themselves at their highest level of ability. The leader's task becomes one of making available as many progressive choices as possible, so that the child can choose, succeed, build self-confidence and learn. Thus leaders play a vital part in helping the child to become free to learn.

MODIFICATIONS

Because rushing may interfere with the actual development of memory (if a child must hurry, she or he may simply follow others rather than try to remember), it might be helpful to pause (time to remember) before the signal to start when this activity is first introduced. Another technique used with the pause is to ask the children to close their eyes as soon as they think they remember which action to use. Those children who can't remember can take clues from the rest of the group when they start to move. Also you will have a better idea of who is having difficulty. Begin with only a few signals and add to them as the group becomes ready.

Basic action signing used by the deaf can replace other signals, a step that adds useful learning material to the activity. Your local library or society for the deaf has basic signing books available.

REINFORCEMENT OF LEARNED INFORMATION

7

Recently it has been found that some children use hearing as their primary mode of learning; others, seeing; others, doing or imagining. I feel that there are probably also smellers, tasters, touchers, and those who receive input in ways still unknown to us or in combinations as individual as fingerprints and personalities. Some children are concrete in their thinking processes; others are abstract. If our goal is to facilitate learning, then it behooves us to make that which we wish the child to comprehend available in whatever form or combination of forms the child can best handle.

Could air, air molecules, movement of air, and air resistance be more comprehensible for some children if incorporated into parachute play, balloon activities, and/ or "Ping Pong Blow," "Paper Plate Play," or flying paper airplanes? Could a sequence, spelling, math or other basic information be learned more thoroughly through the inclusion of related activity?

The selection and modification of movement activities for the reinforcement of specific learned information requires creativity and adaptability. The activities in this chapter may give you some helpful examples. Appendix B on p. 199 includes some additional activities that may hold promise for your group.

TRUE OR FALSE

The children sit in chairs, and a true-or-false question is asked. Time is allowed for the children to decide their answers. On "ready . . . go" all must move to the right of their chairs if the answer is true, or to the left if the answer is false. Then the answer is given and all sit down again. Another question is asked. You may want to allow the children to ask for clarification of the question and/or the answer.

Attention span and concentration, listening skills, release of tension and excessive energy continous movement and participation; total group involvement; rapid feedback

Self-control directing oneself independently

Development of thinking processes decision-making process

Physical fitness see fitness modification

COMMENTS AND SUGGESTIONS

This might be an excellent opportunity for a rapid check of what the children do or do not understand about a given topic. It is also a chance for the children to learn from their own answers since the feedback is clear and immediate.

Don't be too concerned if some children move after they see another child move. Remember the objective is learning or review, not beating someone else or embarrassing a child. Encourage independent decision making by making it all right to learn from one's mistakes. Being aware of an error can increase learning whereas being afraid or embarrassed by an error can reduce it.

MODIFICATIONS

For fitness or to increase the level of activity, have the children do some active movement (e.g., running in place, hopping) after choosing whether to move left or right.

Using the above modification you could have the children move in two different ways, one for true and one for false—thus eliminating the move to left or right.

Write a spelling word (either correctly or incorrectly spelled). Ask the children to respond according to whether it is spelled correctly or not. Then ask them to help you correct the word if it is incorrectly spelled.

For a quiet activity have the children stay in their seats, heads down, and eyes closed. Ask them to raise their right hands if an answer is true and left hands if false. The answer can then be announced. The children put their hands down, and another question is asked.

CLAP YOUR NAME

The children begin clapping the syllables of their first name. Listening, they seek others who are clapping a similar pattern. They form groups.

Perceptual motor development pattern recognition, auditory discrimination; audio figure and ground discrimination; *selecting* a particular pattern of sound

Attention span and concentration individual involvement; personal identity

Listening skills careful, selective listening

Self-control movement

Development of thinking processes analysis; critical thinking; pattern recognition

Reinforcement of learned information syllabic awareness and discrimination

Social growth some sense of belonging to a group; identity with others (may be especially important for the shy or withdrawn child)

COMMENTS AND SUGGESTIONS

This game might be helpful for a new child as it gives an identity and encourages relating to others.

Some children will need help. Try to observe closely those who seem hesitant or inconsistent. Feel free to move among them.

You may also discover a child who needs a hearing examination. Children who have difficulty dividing words into syllables may not be hearing part of the word. A child may have learned to cope with this limitation to some degree by taking whatever pieces of a word he or she can hear and guessing at the meaning. This handicap may sometimes mask itself by making a child seem inattentive and slow.

If you think a group of children may not accept the responsibility of not bumping into one another, you could play "Cross Over" first.

Use last names.

Assign words (other than names) with different numbers of syllables, and have the children form groups. Have them see if their word fits with those of other members.

Assign two well-known songs. Ask the children to clap the song and find a like group.

Have the children clap the syllables in the month of their birth.

Ask them to clap how many brothers and/or sisters they have.

Ask questions that have one-word answers. Have the children clap the answer and then ask them to say it in unison after clapping it a second time.

In moving and clapping activities you may have the children close their eyes.

See "Gesture Name Game."

MOVING MATH

Give any math problem and ask the children to move as quickly as possible into groups the size of the answer. The players are to continue to regroup until all but one group has formed the answer. This group may then raise the number of hands needed to bring the body and hand count to the correct answer. Raising a hand can also show other children where additional players are needed.

To encourage the reinforcement of the related math concepts, you could include a challenge that allows you to ask any child in any group to give both the problem and the answer or to answer a question about the problem.

Attention span and concentration players *needed* for groups; children drawn in

Release of tension and excessive energy movement; help from others (learning without sense of failure)

Self-control tied to a group

Development of thinking processes and reinforcement of learned information modifying activity may improve thinking and learning in particular group

Social growth sense of being needed; cooperation

Physical fitness see modification

COMMENTS AND SUGGESTIONS

This activity encourages everyone to be involved in working toward the answer.
Reinforcement is available both visually and in action.
Various levels of ability are encouraged to help each other.
Children receive immediate feedback.
You are free to observe who is having difficulty and what type of social interaction occurs in your group.
You might encourage groups to prepare all their members with possible answers to your challenge question.
You may need to evaluate the *effectiveness* of the challenge. It may slow your group down too much. The pacing of an activity, whether it should be played in part or in total, and for how long are all best determined by the individual working with a particular group. There are no set rules.
It might be helpful in some excitable groups to:

- try a series in *slow motion*
- work on body control; avoid bumping (you might want to consider "Cross Over" as a preliminary activity)

Perhaps you can think of a way to deal with fractions.
See "Body-Built Letters and Numbers."
This activity can also be used to divide your group into *specific* sized groups for other activities.

MODIFICATIONS

This variation should improve physical fitness. Each child works alone, and the problems should have large answers. You may let the children work with pencil and paper and then at a signal stand and give the answer in unison. The children respond by performing some predetermined movement—such as marching in place, doing jumping jacks, running in place, clapping, or hopping in place—as they count aloud to the answer, sitting down immediately after they have reached it.
Perhaps you think of other enjoyable ways to reinforce math concepts.

EXCHANGE TAG

This is a basic game form to which you can add signals that are most appropriate for your group (see examples under "Possibilities").
The group is divided roughly in half, with each half taking a position on one of two parallel lines. Each player is assigned a signal. The same signal can be assigned to one or more players on one or both lines. At the signal the designated player(s) try to move (exchange) to the opposite line while not being tagged. One player is asked to be the signal caller and first tagger. This player's position is approximately midway between the two lines.

The tagger will try to see how many players can be tagged in the process of the exchange. The first person to be tagged could become the caller–tagger (using only one tagger each time) for the next exchange, or all players tagged could help the original tagger on the next exchange (whichever seems best for your group).

Perceptual motor development body and space awareness; estimation of distance

Attention span and concentration break from routine (play can be used as an extrinsic reward until children also become aware of the intrinsic pleasure of other types of involvement)

Listening skills encourages listening

Development of thinking processes recalling information or learning; decision making; developing strategies

Reinforcement of learned information reinforcing material selected by leader

Physical abilities maneuvering one's body around obstacles

COMMENTS AND SUGGESTIONS

As many signals as you desire can be assigned.
Encourage the children to open up their lines so that the runners can run across them without bumping into anyone.
Depending upon your choice of signals, you might want to have answer cards prepared for runners to hold up in front of them and a call card for the caller–tagger. This step ensures information coverage, visual check of answers by all players, and participation by everyone. Often the children can make these signal cards themselves.

A fast way to divide a group in half is to ask everyone to get a partner (anyone close). Then ask that one go to one line and the other to the other line.

MODIFICATIONS

If you have limited space, you could require fast walking rather than running. Walking is defined as a heel-to-toe pattern of floor contact on each step.

This game could be done on carpets (see "Carpet Activities").

If you wish to first play without special learning signals so the children can learn the basic game, simply ask each line to count off by threes or fours and call a number for the exchange.

POSSIBILITIES

Assign answers to the questions you will ask about each category.

HISTORY (presidents)
- presidents after Lincoln
- American president in office at beginning of World War II
- presidents who died in office

MATH
- 2 + 2 = ?
- 12 ÷ 4 = ?
- all numbers divisible by 3
- ¼ divided by ½

SPELLING
- distribute frequently misspelled words leaving out letters that cause difficulty; e.g.,oc_asion; le_sure; hippot_mus

COLORS
- each child is given a particular color

ANIMAL CHARACTERISTICS (give animal names to players)
- walks on four feet
- lays eggs

- lives in jungle
- has fur

STAY OPEN-MINDED ABOUT CREATIVE POSSIBILITIES; MEET YOUR GROUP'S NEEDS.

SHOW ME THE TIME

Have the children stand and face the clock (wall clock or paper practice clock). The leader announces a certain time and asks the children to show that time by reaching their arms as far as possible in the appropriate directions.
Let the children have time to check the correctness of their attempt (visual feedback from others) and then give the next time call.

Perceptual motor development recognizing patterns; directionality; laterality; duplication of movement

Attention span and concentration continous participation; in unison with group

Listening skills listening helps participation (you can also encourage an "eyes closed" challenge)

Development of thinking processes pattern recognition; translation from verbal to action; immediate visual feedback

Reinforcement of learned information practice in telling time; immediate feedback and self-evaluation

Physical abilities duplication of movement

Physical fitness stretching shoulder girdle

COMMENTS AND SUGGESTIONS

You might want to emphasize reaching, since stretching can help relax the children. Many learning activities drop the head forward. This type of activity could reinforce good body alignment. Be specific about the orientation of the clock (mirror image) or the confusion of reverse time may occur. Specify by some examples in which the children follow your lead.

This may be a good time to observe and diagnose problems in spatial awareness or in telling time.

I would encourage self-evaluation through observation of others rather than initial correction by you, since a great deal of learning can occur by this process; it is more immediate and perhaps less time consuming. If you notice a child who is unable to utilize self-evaluation and is continuing to make errors, you might want to work with this child individually later to try to analyze the source of the problem. If the child merely needs practice, another child who can tell time could play this game with this child.

The children could hold a pencil or some extension in one hand to designate the longer minute hand. Some groups are able to show the shorter hour hand by bending their elbows.

MODIFICATIONS

Later you may wish to have the children work without the assistance of the wall clock. Or they could close their eyes, which encourages good listening and more independent thinking.

"Arrows" in its simplest form might be considered a preliminary to this activity. Draw a series of arrows pointing up, down, right, and left. Have the children go through the series, pointing with both arms in the direction of the designated arrow.

Advanced modifications of "Arrows":

- Have the children say a direction (up, down, left, right) as they point.
- Have them point in the opposite direction of the designated arrow.

See "Follow Me" as a possible preliminary. Have the children take a position and then raise the question, "What time is this?"

MAGIC CARPET

Using pieces of colored construction paper, place those colors you wish to reinforce or review around the floor. Have the children move around the floor. As you call a color the children are to move to that color. If there is room, all the children should try to stand on the called color. If there is a limited amount of room, all should try to find ways to help each other touch that color in some way.

Perceptual motor development body control

Attention span and concentration movement; being alert

Release of tension and excessive energy movement

Self-control sharing

Reinforcement of learned information learning colors

Social growth sharing space, cooperating; being responsible not to bump into others

Physical abilities body control

COMMENTS AND SUGGESTIONS

Have several pieces of each color or use the connected line modification. All children should be able to get on or touch the answer in some way.

The activity could be made more personal by adding a "favorite color" call.

You might start the children in a rapid walk to determine if the material will slip and cause a hazard. If so, try the second modification given below.

See "Cooperative Musical Chairs" and "All Aboard" to help the children learn to share.

MODIFICATIONS

Use other concepts: numbers for math answers, states (geography), etc.

The colors could be on tables, hanging on walls, etc. The children must touch and remain in touch with a particular answer until the next signal is given.

The children could hold the hand of anyone wearing a called color. Others could then hold a free hand of a connected child. This might result in long lines all around the room (connected line).

You could ask questions that are answered by colors (e.g. "When you mix blue and yellow you get . . . ?). The children move to the color that is the answer.

It might be interesting to add mood questions, e.g., "What color do you feel is a sad color, a happy color, a quiet color, a fast color, a rainy day color?" Remember there are no right answers to these questions, but they do give children personal choices. This could be a tag game on the order of "Exchange Tag" or

"Safe From the Sharks." The first child tagged becomes "it" for the next round.

You could develop the basic format of this activity to meet the needs of your children.

NINE SQUARE HOPSCOTCH

Because the floor pattern (see Figure 7-1 on p. 146) is used by one individual at a time, you may choose to have several different patterns. A child hops on one foot from one square to another.

Perceptual motor development balance, spatial awareness; body control; laterality; directionality; pattern recognition

Development of thinking processes thinking and doing (application); making rapid decisions; translating using memory; recognizing patterns; sequencing; motor planning; following directions; solving problems

Reinforcement of learned information material should be selected by adult leader (see suggestions)

Physical abilities dynamic (moving) and static balance

Physical fitness cardiorespiratory exercise (if long enough); leg development (children should be encouraged to use the nonpreferred leg)

A pattern with blank squares could be used in several ways:

- hopping from blank to blank while calling out a set of multiples: 2–4–6–8–etc., 9–18–27–36–etc.
- spelling words
- reciting the alphabet
- counting number of hops without a miss
- hopping out answers to math problems given by partner

You could use differently lettered squares:

- spelling certain words called from a prepared list (two children could work alone)
- spelling as many words as possible
- one child spelling a word while second child hops it
- hopping child must then determine the word
- each child finding a new word in pattern and hopping it; others guessing what it is

Encourage children to use the nonpreferred leg also.

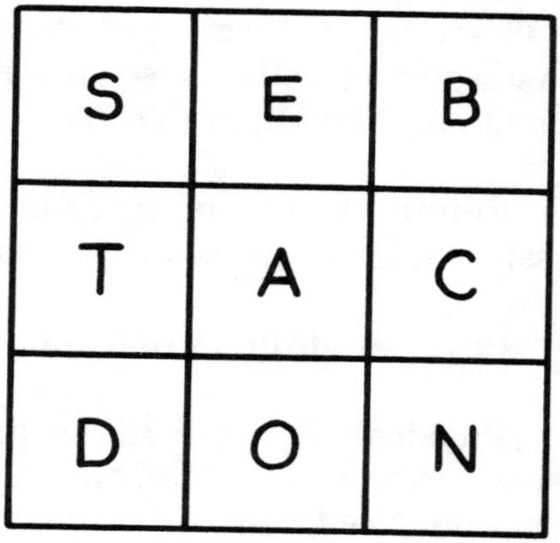

S	E	B
T	A	C
D	O	N

Figure 7–1

If material (cloth) is available and can be used safely, several patterns could be developed. These can be easily stored and used in various locations. Removal of shoes tends to reduce noise, laundry, and wear. For donations of material, let some people know of your need and ask for their suggestions.

MODIFICATIONS

Study the pattern and try to develop new possibilities to meet the particular needs of your children.

SOCIAL
GROWTH

8

Humans are gregarious, tending to group and function together. This human characteristic does not, however, insure the skills required to do this effectively. Today we are finding that our next step in human evolution may, of necessity, have to be an emotional or social one, in which individuals learn to interact more effectively with each other.

Children need opportunities in which they can safely carry out massive social interactions, where they can experience others' responses and become aware of their own feelings.

Play is an important opportunity to safely risk, test, and adjust one's social behavior; at the same time it can improve one's physical abilities, which may allow one to enter more comfortably into additional activities.

For additional related activities, see the index.

All children have partners. One partner closes his or her eyes (robot). The other partner tells the robot how to move in specific ways (forward, backward, left, right, stop, go, etc.) so that the robot can progress around obstacles and on to preset goal.

Perceptual motor development spatial awareness; kinesthetic awareness; motor planning

Attention span and concentration no visual cues; dependency on one source of information

Listening skills listening and interpreting becomes means to success

Self-control bombardment of stimuli reduced; by not making an issue of peeking, *the child* may progressively cope with self-control

Development of thinking processes interpreting information; translating directions into accurate action; analyzing situation; estimating distances; generating alternative solutions; expressing information

Social growth accepting responsibility for another; effective verbal expression; leadership; trusting; risking; accepting help from another; following

Physical abilities motor planning; balance; greater reliance on vestibular (inner ear; contributes to balance) and kinesthetic systems

COMMENTS AND SUGGESTIONS

Anything can be used as an obstacle.

Don't be upset if some children feel that they must peek. It may take them awhile to trust their partners or feel comfortable with their eyes closed. Peeking is merely a needed coping process for some children as they take progressively more difficult risks. Usually as the children become more comfortable, peeking will decrease and not peeking will become a challenge. If the children are peeking to win, it may be that winning is being stressed too much. You might want to encourage cooperation rather than competition, and modify the activity accordingly.

Since trust is involved you may want to let the children choose their partners for the first episode.

Keep an eye open for an endangered "robot"; not all children lead well.

Beginning with only a few robots may result in less confusion until the children become more proficient. With many groups a demonstration first might prove helpful.

MODIFICATIONS

"Happy Landing": A "dock worker" directs the "boat" (partner) to a chair and helps the partner sit down safely. As in "Robot," the partners do not touch. The boat may feel for the chair, *if necessary*.

Increase the number and/or difficulty of the obstacles.

Instead of words partners can use only predetermined sounds to specify various directions.

Have robots without partners. The robot buzzes or hums and moves *slowly* toward a second source of sound (wood blocks hit together, bell, etc.). The object is to reach the goal without colliding with another robot. Collision deactivates the robots, who must then "freeze" as they continue to hum but not move. They are now obstacles to be avoided by still active robots. Because the inactive robots may create an impassable barrier, the second sound may have to be relocated during the activity. Some of the children will be needed to help the robots avoid stationary hazards. These persons may *gently* turn robots away from obstacles.

COOPERATIVE MUSICAL CHAIRS

The children move around in all available space. When the sound or music is stopped, all the children find a chair to sit on. All the children must sit down, so if the number of chairs is inadequate, they must be shared. When everyone is seated the music is started again. The number of chairs can be reduced while the music is playing. As the music stops there are even fewer chairs to seat the group. The challenge is to see if the group can continue to seat all the players even as the number of chairs decreases. What is the fewest possible chairs needed by the group?

Perceptual motor development simple auditory awareness; body and space relationships; motor planning; spatial estimation; laterality

Listening skills alert listening

Self-control cooperation needed

Social growth one of a series of activities specifically developed to emphasize and encourage cooperative group interaction; see *Cooperative Sports and Games* Terry Orlick, New York: Pantheon, 1978.

COMMENTS AND SUGGESTIONS

Thanks to Terry Orlick and others who are making play alternatives available to us.

Chairs do not have to be lined up in a formal manner. They could be randomly scattered and can include all types.

Older children can play "All Aboard" or "Team on a T-Shirt."

This is a good opportunity for children to listen to various forms of music (from a radio, record player, small tape cassette recorder, etc.).

Volume control is an alternative to turning the machine on and off.

Chairs must be sufficiently sturdy.

This game might be followed by "All Aboard."

If you see a child who seems to relate to the other children's movement rather than to the music, try to evaluate whether the child is not auditorily aware, has a hearing problem, or is slow in reaction or movement time. You can play games that involve these factors or request appropriate tests.

MODIFICATIONS

See "Magic Carpets" (color discrimination).

The basic concept in cooperation is for all involved to overcome a common problem or to obtain a difficult goal. When we accomplish that, we have won, and the only the loser is the problem.

Perhaps you could create or convert movement activities to cooperative learning experiences.

WAVE THE OCEAN

Place chairs in a close circle. Leave one chair empty. When the leader calls "flow right,' the child with the empty chair to his or her right slides into that chair and each player follows. When the leader says "flow left," the opposite occurs. The object is to "flow" as rapidly and as smoothly as possible.

Perceptual motor development laterality

Attention span and concentration group movement; (extremely difficult not to pay attention since each player affected by player to either side)

Listening skills verbal cues (see also sound modification)

Release of tension and excessive energy interactive flow; gentle pushing; opportunity to move; action a bit absurd; laughter; change of pace

Self-control group cooperation

Development of thinking processes receiving verbal, visual, or sometimes tactile cues; quick interpretation

Social growth gentle touching; feeling of being part of a group

Physical abilities timing; motor planning; balance; moving with, rather than resisting, an outside force

COMMENTS AND SUGGESTIONS

Sturdy chairs without arms are needed.
Start slow since it may take the players a little while to get the idea and begin to work smoothly together.
Later, as the group becomes proficient, shift the flow more often as a challenge to their attention and listening ability.
It might help if the leader made calls near the empty chair.
This activity may be particularly good for the shy or withdrawn child. Although each child is a real part of the group and is important to its functioning, there is little possibility of individual fault. Lots of gentle bumping occurs, which allows for contact with others without focusing on touching. It must also be realized that some shy and withdrawn children (or others) may not be ready for this type of activity. It may still be beyond their present point of interactive ability or comfort. If you are concerned about a particular child you might wish to develop a progression that will allow for more comfortable change. If you are not worried about a particular child, but a child or children may be uncomfortable with the activity, consider giving any child the opportunity not to participate. Also try to make it possible for the child to join in if his or her feelings change.

MODIFICATION

The leader could try to sit in any empty chair that is available during the flow. If the leader successfully sits in the empty chair, the flow stops and a new leader is designated.
After the group is functioning fairly well, the leader could also

call a flow that is already in progress; thus a new element of thought and decision is added.

A modification could be created by using sounds rather than words (see "Sounds to Move By").

"Moving Boxes" is a difficult modification and requires real teamwork. The group stands in one or several close boxlike formations. Four instructions may be called: right, left, forward, or backward. The group must move *together*. Go slow at first. The groups can figure out strategies to make it work (see "Many Move" and "Trolley").

You might like to try combining "North, East, South, and West" with "Moving Boxes."

CLOTHES RELAY

Divide the group into teams (four to a team allows all to play without too much standing around). Each team is given one or more pieces of clothing. At a signal each team dresses one of its members. This person moves as quickly as possible around a designated spot and returns to the team place. Then the next team member is dressed by the team. This process is continued until all have finished. The team indicates completion by sitting down and raising hands.

Perceptual motor development body awareness; body image; coordination; spatial awareness (relationships); body perceptions (for this purpose you might eliminate the competitive relay)

Release of tension and excessive energy funny absurdity; excitement; opportunity to move

Self-control need only be at bare minimum but still contributes to goal.

Social growth helping each other; hurrying but still being considerate of the individual; working as a loosely organized team; laughing at and with each other

COMMENTS AND SUGGESTIONS

Try to equalize the clothes between teams.
You may wish to specify ground rules, such as all sweater buttons must be buttoned; scarf must be tied on head; galoshes must be buckled.
Children with real difficulty in body perceptions may benefit from a somewhat similar activity. The objective would be to *completely* dress each teammate (approved by leader) without the time-rush factor. All team members must help. Perhaps a big shirt with buttons, one pair of large shorts, and a pair of tie-on shoes could be used.

MODIFICATIONS

"Sweatshirt Relay" (large shirts best): Only one sweatshirt is given to a team. One member has on the sweatshirt. The next teammate grasps hands with the sweatshirted teammate while the other two members of the team turn the sweatshirt inside out, moving it over and off the first player as they pull it over and onto the second player. This player immediately takes the hands of a third member of the team, and the process continues. As soon as the first player has the shirt on again, all sit down. In some cases *care* will have to be taken to assure that *only* the sweatshirt is pulled off the player. This may need to be a ground rule.

HUMAN KNOT

Usually ten or twelve participants work together. The group stands shoulder to shoulder in a circle. All should reach into the middle and take a hand in each of theirs. The group then tries to untangle themselves without letting go of each other's hands. The hands can be pivoted within each other.

Attention span and concentration entire group linked together and working on a single problem

Self-control hands are linked; must remain with group, listen to others' ideas, try to contribute, deal with frustrations

Development of thinking processes problem solving; dealing with complex spacial relationships, cause and effect, and trial and error

Social growth social interaction and evaluation (some leaders initiate discussions following the activity)

COMMENTS AND SUGGESTIONS

This is a learning situation in which a player may make evaluative decisions about which interaction behaviors seem most effective and change their own personal behavior accordingly.

It may help if each player tries to get the hands of two different participants.

Large groups (twenty-four to twenty-seven) have been known to succeed as a "Human Knot," but with children or beginners it might be better to keep the group small.

Large groups may be split into smaller groups who work separately.

This activity requires perseverance so it may not be appropriate for a young child or a group that becomes easily frustrated. If you decide to play this game with such children, you may want to reduce the group to five or fewer.

It is possible that a knot cannot be untangled. Then you may have a "knot-aid," i.e., a single breaking of hands. These hands are then rejoined in a more advantageous position, and the group tries again to untangle the knot.

If you have begun to enjoy the use of games I would encourage you to seek out a copy of *The New Games Book,* edited by Andrew Fluegelman, Dolphin/Doubleday, 1976.

CAR AND DRIVER

The children have partners. One (the driver) stands behind the other (the car). The players designated as cars close their eyes. The drivers direct, stop, and start the cars with only their hands, which are placed upon their partners' shoulders. Players later change positions.

Begin by having the drivers direct the cars around some obstacle. Then as experience is gained, cars can cross each other's paths. Right of way should be observed (the person on the right). Also the cars may make a quiet beeping sound. From this basic beginning feel free to create and elaborate according to the needs of your group.

Attention span and concentration constant involvement

Release of tension and excessive energy sense of relief from other stress

Self-control trust; responsibility for another (self-control can get out of hand)

Reinforcement of learned information concept of right of way

Social growth trust; responsibility for another; leader or follower role; not bumping others; sensitivity to someone else's fear or hesitancy

COMMENTS AND SUGGESTIONS

"Cross Over" and "Robot" may be good preliminary activities for this one.
The cars may feel more comfortable if they are allowed to put their arms out in front of them.
As a final calming activity you might want to play the humming "Cross Over" modification, using a *quiet* beep-beep. Any players touching are broken down in accidents, and although they can continue to quietly beep, they must remain still. The objective of the activity could be to begin on one wall and try to move to a particular sound—bell, spoons, etc.—that could be either stationary or moving.
Skill rather than speed or winning should be stressed.

MODIFICATIONS

Place participants on four sides of an open space. Have two of the sides opposite each other go; then the other two sides. Later all four sides can drive at once. If two cars touch, an accident has occurred and they cannot move from the scene (another obstacle for other drivers to drive around). You can create the role of a person who touches the car (report and repair), which then is free to move again.

ALL ABOARD (TEAM ON A T-SHIRT)

Have a designated surface (cloth, T-shirt, flat board, tree stump, tires, platform, etc.) upon which all members of the group must stand at the same time (balance on one foot is permitted). To be an official success, the group needs to stay in balance for a ten-second count (one thousand and one, one thousand and two, etc., to one thousand and ten).

Perceptual motor development body awareness; kinesthetic awareness; balance

Release of tension and excessive energy concentration on purpose; group problem solving; struggling for group success

Self-control making contributions; being patient; persevering

Development of thinking processes possible recognition of counterbalance and relationships; some awareness of cause and effect

Reinforcement of learned information could be related to the study of balance or equalization

Social growth contributing and listening (sharing ideas); being patient with others, helping and being helped

Physical abilities balance

COMMENTS AND SUGGESTIONS

This and several other good group problem-solving activities have been brought together in a book entitled, *Cowstails and Cobras* by Karl Rohnke (available through Project Adventure, P.O. Box 157, Hamilton, Massachusetts, 01936).

"Human Knot" might be a good preliminary activity.

Give some thought to how many should be in a group. It might help to have material for several groups; then as they become proficient you can make the group larger or the standing area smaller.

If you use a supporting surface above the ground (e.g., platform, cutoff tree stump), be sure it is sturdy and that there are no hazardous obstacles around it.

Surfaces that could roll or move out from under a group are usually too hazardous.

If your group enjoys this type of activity look into "Creative Teeter-Totter."

Problem solving can sometimes be enhanced by creating a story around the specific problem (e.g., a tidal wave is passing over the surface of the earth and the only way the group can be saved is by being on board the All Aboard when it arrives. It is due in two minutes and thirty-two seconds).

MODIFICATIONS

Almost anything of adequate size can be used for standing on as long as it is safe and affords the group a problem to solve.

You can also simply use an area marked off on the floor or ground.

Instead of standing on something, all the members of the group could try to touch something, like a book or a specific person.

This variation requires less touching and may be preferred by some groups.

Use the above modification, but as the players touch an object they cannot touch anyone else; this is much more difficult.

A long board could be used.

If your group becomes proficient, they may want to be timed to see if they can beat the clock in completing the task.

BIG TURTLE

Two or more children (on their hands and knees) are covered by a sheet-like cloth. (If no cloth is available, the players could close their eyes. The children try to travel in any direction together. At the first attempt the children may go in all different directions and the cloth may fall to the ground. Be patient and encourage them to try again. The objective of the activity is to work together to move as a unit.

Perceptual motor development body and space relationships; spatial awareness and relationships

Attention span and concentration children are under a cover and have little else to distract them; focus on solution (as a group) may be somewhat diversified until they learn to work together

Self-control communication, planning, and compromise; immediate and obvious feedback; sustained involvement

Development of thinking processes exploring possibilities; generating alternatives; making decisions; thinking out a plan; ongoing evaluation

Social growth cooperating (efforts toward a common goal); leading and following; adapting and compromising

COMMENTS AND SUGGESTIONS

Thanks to Terry Orlick, *Cooperative Sports and Games* (Pantheon) for the basic idea of "Big Turtle."
This type of activity can be approached in many ways. You may find it helpful to specify where or how far the children are to try to go on the first trials (e.g., across the room, to any wall). You may want to consider how you will set up the activity for your group, e.g., how much structure and how many children under the cloth each time.
The way you present and structure the problem may have interesting results. What are you seeking to accomplish? Do you feel you should be patient and observe, or should the problem be made more specific? Would the frustration and tolerance level of the particular group of children make a difference? Should you establish progressively challenging goals, or can the children do that?
You should be aware of how warm it gets under the cloth when the children are huddled together.
Competition between cooperating groups is not a part of this activity. I believe this is deliberate in Dr. Orlick's work, and I would recommend his books highly.

MODIFICATIONS

If you wish to stress spatial awareness you could establish a specific spot to which the turtle attempts to travel. If awareness of space is the objective, rather than cooperation, individual children could work alone.
You could give direction to the turtle in various ways, depending on your objective (e.g. moving without outside cues; moving

toward a sound; having a child who sees give assistance in some way; following some tactile cues).

Children connected in some way (holding on to a piece of rope or cloth) could close their eyes or use blindfolds.

Some older groups might feel that being on hands and knees was childish. Perhaps this activity could be done standing up, in which case you may want to change its name.

This activity has creative possibilities. How could you modify it to meet the various needs of your group?

ALASKAN BASEBALL

The batting team lines up one behind another. The fielding team scatters all over the area where the ball may be hit. The first player on the batting team propels the ball (hits, throws, or kicks) out into the field and begins circling his or her team members. Each time the batter passes the front of the line, a run is scored. The batter continues to run. The first member of the fielding team who gets to the ball picks it up, while all other teammates line up immediately behind this player. The ball is passed over their heads, one to another. When the last player in the line receives the ball, he or she runs to the front of the line and all sit down as they yell "stop." At this call no more runs can be scored by the running batter.

Attention span and concentration learning to attend and concentrate selectively; movement and involvement for fielding team, but batting team tends to wait (see last modification)

Self-control working together as a unit

Development of thinking processes constantly evaluating evolving situation; making appropriate application of ongoing input; using individual and team strategies

Social growth participating as member of a team; sharing; awaiting turn; compromising; contributing; leading and following; playing fair; belonging; doing one's best

Physical abilities catching and hitting; speed (reduced reaction and movement time)

POSSIBLE PROGRESSION

Play as a relay, with each team member circling the team one and a half times and taking a place at the end of the line (the team will have to keep moving up one step as each runner finishes to keep the team in place).

Play as a relay, with the team passing the ball over their heads. The last person in line runs to the front of the line as he or she receives the ball and starts the ball overhead again until the entire team is finished.

Scatter challenge: Two teams scatter over the available space. On a signal they try to organize themselves behind the teammate with the ball and pass the ball overhead to see which group can finish first.

Demonstrate the regulation game in slow motion.

Play the regulation game.

COMMENTS AND SUGGESTIONS

This is a good playground or outdoor activity. A rubber utility ball (ten to twelve inches) can be used. If a large space is not available you can use a beachball or yarnball.

Encourage players to consider strategies if they play this game over several play periods:

- where to place the hit
- how to get the batter around the batting team more times
- how the fielding team can work together more effectively

Do not bother to change ends of the playing area. If at all possible let the teams bat and field in their end. Changing ends is a slow process that consumes important play time and is unnecessary in this activity.

MODIFICATIONS

Use something to set the ball on such as a batting tee (see "Making Equipment at Little or No Cost," p. 201.).
You could have fly balls or even first bounces count as an out, *but* you are reducing the amount of action and success.
An enjoyable and effective way to play this game is to have the two teams alternate turns at batting. The playing formation allows this to be done without changing ends of the playing area.

MANY MOVE

The children (in groups of two, three, four, or five) form a line, placing hands on the waist or shoulders of the person in front of them. Now they try to move forward in unison.

Perceptual motor development laterality; directionality; duplication of movement; motor planning; spatial awarenes; timing

Attention span and concentration close connection with others; immediacy of possible solution

Self-control function as part of group

Development of thinking processes generation of alternative solutions; group decision making; careful observation; estimation of time and distance (extrapolation); motor planning; constant evaluation

Social growth working with others toward a common goal (cooperation, teamwork); making suggestions; expressing oneself effectively; listening to and interacting with others' ideas

Physical abilities timing (pacing); rhythm; duplication of movement; reading another's movement

COMMENTS AND SUGGESTIONS

If this game is played as a relay, players all drop their hands (when all have reached the goal line), turn around and put their hands on the person now in front of them (thus having reversed the line), and move back to their original starting point. Trying to turn groups of three, four, or five is a difficult and awkward task (especially in limited space). Be aware that competition before skill and cooperation have been developed may reduce the development of these components.

Perhaps it would be wise to let the children work on how they can move best together.

If the children have previously played "Mirroring," this activity may be easier for them because of their developed ability to follow another's movements and timing.

You might start with two players working together, then three, four, and five. You might want to let the children simply wander around the room until they become accustomed to moving together.

Have the children try to play without touching each other (very skillful).

Have all but the leader close their eyes.

See "Wave the Ocean," "Trolley," and "Moving Boxes."

TROLLEY

Two strips of cloth are laid side by side on the floor. Starting about three feet from the front end, all participants (two to six) step onto the cloth. All left feet are placed on one strip, all right feet on the other. The first player (conductor) then reaches down and takes the extra length of cloth and pulls it up to his or her thighs. All players then try to synchronize their steps to move forward.

Perceptual motor development temporal awareness

Attention span and concentration and release of tension traps attention and concentration, but probably won't carry over to other situations; creates sense of singleness of purpose

Self-control experience in self-control with an enjoyable objective

170

Development of thinking processes analysis; generation of alternative solutions; synthesis; motor planning; appropriate application of information; careful observation, evaluation, and adjustment

Social growth listening to others; contributing; expressing oneself effectively; affecting and being part of group decisions; functioning as a unit to accomplish a purpose; failing and succeeding with others; evaluating as group

Physical abilities timing (rhythm and synchronizing pace with others); adjusting to outside forces; balancing

COMMENTS AND SUGGESTIONS

Needed are cloth strips approximately four to six inches wide and sufficiently long to allow two to six participants, one behind another, to stand on them with three feet of cloth to be held to the thigh by the conductor.

The passengers on the cloth strips usually automatically take hold of the waist of the person in front of them—which helps timing and balance.

The greater the number of passengers the more difficult the problem. You may want to start with only a few passengers and allow the children to add passengers as they feel ready.

Again, a good creative story can enhance problem solving. Perhaps the players could be captives. The floor could be charged in a special way, and the cloth or plank could have been treated to neutralize this charge. The players' task is to try to escape over the involved area to safety.

See "Many Move," which could be a preliminary activity.

MODIFICATIONS

Newspaper strips could be used for two or three participants, but they may need to be reinforced with masking tape.

Figure 8–1

Some players have used wooden planks (approximately two inches by four inches by six feet) with hand ropes set into a "trolley" for each participant.

Long carpet strips can be used, and perhaps a pair of old trousers or coveralls.

PHYSICAL NEEDS

9

Physical skills and abilities can be developed through appropriate experiences and practice. A child can be helped to gain skills such as:

- body control and adaptability
- ability to monitor a situation and respond accordingly
- functioning effectively under stress
- those used in basic sports
- manual dexterity
- improved accuracy
- object manipulation
- alertness
- timing
- adjusting to outside forces
- agility
- ability to stop and start quickly

Movement activities can also contribute to various factors that improve a child's level of physical fitness:

- cardiovascular endurance
- respiratory endurance
- muscular endurance
- shoulder girdle development
- abdominal development
- flexibility, range of motion
- ability to relax
- proper body alignment

Both physical abilities and fitness can make a child feel more competent, be more successful, and enter social groups with some degree of comfort. "The personal satisfaction that a child derives from being able to do something well is an important factor in his concept of *himself. In other words, motor development—as well as mental development—is vital from the standpoint of mental health."*[1]

Bela Mittelman (Department of Psychiatry, New York University College of Medicine) has noted both the negative and positive potential of the physical in his study of motility. *"Inadequate motor performance leading to derogatory comments or rejection by parents or other children may be one of the most significant sources of the feeling of inadequacy."*[2] Whereas *" . . . adequate solution of the motor problem is attended by joy and leads to repetition."*[3]

Movement activities can serve as a source for the development of physical skills and the maintenance of physical fitness and should be selected with this in mind.

[1] Arthur Jersild, *Child Psychology* (Englewood Cliffs, N.J.: Prentice-Hall, Inc., 1968), p. 115.

[2] Bela Mittelman, "Motility in Infants, Children, and Adults," in *Psychoanalytic Studies of the Child*, 9, 1954, p. 167.

[3] *Ibid.*, p. 174.

GUARD THE GOLDEN FLEECE

The golden fleece is placed on the floor in the center of the area. One guard is chosen, who can freeze any other player with a mere touch. All the other players try to steal the golden fleece without being touched. If a player steals the fleece he or she becomes the new guard.

All the players touched must stay frozen until the fleece has been stolen or all players have been frozen. If the guard freezes all players before one can steal the fleece, the guard is declared "outstanding guard" and can select another player as guard.

Perceptual motor development rapid adjusting; responding to continuously changing situation (motor planning and adapting— neuromuscular development)

Attention span and concentration selective attention and involvment;

Release of tension and excessive energy risk; involvement

Development of thinking processes individual, partner, and group strategies; rapid monitoring and reaction; great deal of motor planning

Physical abilities guarding skills; rapid body adjustment; agility; body control; eye, hand, object coordination; dodging; improved reaction time; neuromuscular development

COMMENTS AND SUGGESTIONS

With time, strategies begin to evolve, both individual and cooperative.

As the children become familiar with the activity and are increasingly more skillful, you could divide the group into smaller groups and encourage them to direct their own activity.

MODIFICATIONS

It is fun to play this game indoors on the floor, but it can also be played outside.

Although most groups are challenged by one fleece and one guard, it is possible to add another fleece or guard if you feel it would contribute to the activity. (Remember: a game should be changed *because* it *adds* something to the activity.)

PING-PONG BLOW

Children lie on their stomachs in two lines facing each other. Their hands are placed under their chins and their elbows are extended to their sides, forming a straight line with teammates. A ball is placed between the two lines. Each team tries to blow the ball so that it passes over the opponent's line or touches an opponent in any way.

Release of tension and excessive energy laughing; exercising back and neck muscles

Social growth member of team; avoids personal sense of inadequacy (of being chosen last or responsible for losing game)

Physical fitness upper back and neck exercise; respiratory exercise

Figure 9–1

COMMENTS AND SUGGESTIONS

A Ping-Pong ball or any small, light, roundish object, such as a tissue-paper-rubberband ball, could be used.

If the children are going to be on the floor, it should be clean.

This game can be played on a table top. Nothing but the chin is placed on the table.

This activity might be of particular value for children who are retarded, asthmatic, or physically handicapped, since they sometimes have had limited play opportunity to develop a strong respiratory system. These children frequently suffer from more upper respiratory infections than other children. (See also the respiratory modification in "Paper Plate Play.")

"Ping-Pong Blow" has been played by bed patients in hospitals. The beds are pulled up to a table, the patients are turned on their stomachs, and the game begins. Because these are infrequently used muscles, rest periods will be important and the length of activity may need to be fairly brief during the first several sessions.

A masking tape line may help if children have trouble determining goals.

Perhaps this game should not be played during the flu and cold season.

If the children tend to spit, short straws or straws cut in half may reduce this problem.

MODIFICATIONS

This game can be played with almost any light rolling object. If the object is odd shaped or weighted (like a balloon with a button or bean in it), it might be even more fun. Older children sometimes feel balloons are too childish for them. Blown-out eggs were used originally, and the game was appropriately named "Egg Blow."

For windy students you may have to have a heavier ball or increase the distance between the lines.

You could split the group into smaller groups and have a little round robin tournament.

You could use two objects with one group.

This game can be played one on one.

This could be a golf-like game (blowing object into a practice cup) rather than one of team against team.

The players could blow the ball off the table and try to drop it into a wastepaper basket.

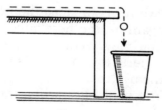

Figure 9–2

LOO K'BAH ZEE (FROM BURMA)

Divide the players into groups of four, five, or six. (Large groups tend to mean too many children are waiting for a turn.)
Each group has a small object (e.g., button, piece of chalk). Indicate who shall start in each group. The other three to five players line up shoulder to shoulder (but not touching), facing the same direction, with their hands held open behind their backs. A player with the object moves from one to another, touching each player's hands. Into one player's hands the object is dropped. This player then jumps forward while the players on either side of the jumper try to reach out and tag him or her. The successful jumper or tagger becomes the next dropper.

Attention span and concentration maintaining alertness and attention without frequent reinforcement; immediate opportunity to try again

Physical abilities improved response time following visual input

COMMENTS AND SUGGESTIONS

The players could change places occasionally so they are standing next to someone different.
If the same people are always selected, ask those who have had two turns to close their hands so they will not receive the object again until others have had a turn.
You may wish to demonstrate with one group and then let the others try. This also allows them to practice organizing themselves.
You could use a line (floor pattern or cracks between boards) to

indicate how far a player must go before he or she is safe. This line need only be out of the reach of the other players.

AFRICAN SIMON SAYS

One child faces all others (or a circle formation could be used). All players raise their arms high over their heads and clap three times. The leader brings one arm down quickly until it is parallel to the floor. All players try to duplicate this movement using the *same* arm as the leader. Allow each leader about three turns.

Perceptual motor development visual acuity (keenness of perception); body awareness; laterality; duplication of movement

Attention span and concentration active involvement; simplicity; singular input; sudden visual stimulus; immediate evaluation; frequency; brevity (concentration not a constant requirement, child can learn about timing high levels of alertness)

Self-control functioning under planned stress

Development of thinking processes rapid monitoring and decision making

Physical abilities body awareness; duplication of movement; improved reaction time

Physical fitness stretching chest muscles

Visual acuity and rapid interpretation are important skills. "Follow Me" might be a good preliminary activity.

This game can be used as a quickbreak. Stretching releases muscular tension.

Periodic stretching of the chest muscles can help prevent rounded shoulders.

MODIFICATIONS

Use other arm movements—to side, elbow bent, etc.

Use arms and a leg

Play "Show Me the Time" with audio but no visual cues.

"Arrows" might be a preliminary activity.

What are your group needs? Can you create modifications to meet these needs?

CARPET ACTIVITIES

Have each child (who is not handicapped) stand upon a piece of carpet. To move a child must "twist" by rotating his or her hips (no "scooting" allowed). The children can now play all kinds of tag and snatch games, relays, hockey-like games, etc.

Perceptual motor development body control (balance and coordination); kinesthetic awareness

Release of tension and excessive energy moving; twisting; stretching; having fun; concentrating

Social growth good for child limited in mobility (see "Comments and Suggestions"); group could discuss physical limitations and their feelings about those who have them

Physical abilities dynamic (moving) balance

Physical fitness abdominal development; vigorous workout; cardiovascular endurance

COMMENTS AND SUGGESTIONS

The carpet strips are approximately five inches by ten inches.
This activity was originally developed to allow an individual who was partially paralyzed and walked with Canadian crutches and leg braces to participate with others. Placing everyone else on carpets somewhat equalized the group. The child could travel on her crutches about as fast as the others could on the rug strips.
Putting the carpet or back side down may depend on your group's level of skill.
Mat backing seems to hold up better than rubberized backing.
The size of the carpet should be changed to meet the needs of your group.
Carpets allow for a great deal of vigorous activity in a small space.

MODIFICATIONS

"Carpet Skiing": To use carpet activities for the very young or less experienced you might try a small piece of carpet under each foot and let them move as if skating or cross-country skiing.

Each of the following could be played on carpets:

Cross Over	Clothes Relay
Snatch the Bacon	Falling off the Log
Safe from the Sharks	Squirrel in the Tree
Exchange Tag	

It is important to use carpets only in activities in which most children are active and not waiting for a turn.

The children could sit on larger pieces of carpet while being pushed or pulled by another.

FREEZE

The players begin to move, slowly at first. They are encouraged to increase activity and type of movements they are using. At the signal "freeze," all players try to become immediately still and hold the frozen position until "melt" is called.

Perceptual motor development body control (balance); kinesthetic awareness; body and space relationships; spatial awareness (estimation and relationships)

Attention span and concentration challenges; need to be alert; ability to hold position

Release of tension and excessive energy concentration; personal involvement; choices; opportunity to take chances

Self-control physical and emotional

Development of thinking processes creating; making decisions

Physical abilities dynamic (moving) and static balance

COMMENTS AND SUGGESTIONS

Body control and balance are important skills. All movement is based upon them, and many serious accidents can be avoided by persons who develop these abilities.

MODIFICATIONS

The activity is done in slow motion. Each player challenges him- or herself with difficult movements.

The children have partners; one moves in slow motion while the other calls the signals.

Play music, like in musical chairs. When the music stops the children freeze. Melt occurs when the music begins again.

As the leader calls freeze and melt, partners move in unison (somewhat like "Mirroring" and "Me and My Shadow") in slow motion.

The children have bean bags on their heads. They all try to move into the most difficult body positions they can create. If a beanbag falls that player is frozen, unless another player, while still participating, can replace the bag on the player's head.

You could add a challenge for any child who wishes to accept it. "Can you hold your position with one or both eyes closed?"

PAPER CUP RELAY

The children form teams of three or four (small teams give more opportunity for each player to move). Each team has a paper cup, which can be balanced on various parts of th body for each relay (e.g., head, forehead, elbow, hand, toe). Each player moves to the designated line and returns to the team. This step continues until all have completed the task. If the cup falls, the player must stop, recover the cup, and go on. Otherwise the cup may not be touched.

Perceptual motor development body awareness; tactile awareness (receiving input from the sense of touch)

Attention span and concentration specific problem requires constant attention

Self-control physical and emotional; child must know limitations

Social growth responsibility to group; sense of belonging to a team; participating within the rules

Physical abilities body control

COMMENTS AND SUGGESTIONS

Because hurrying seems to reduce the possibility of meeting certain valuable objectives (body control and awareness), I have sometimes changed the approach from racing to being able to complete the task, within a given amount of time, with as few spills of the cup as possible. I try to give sufficient time to avoid the need to rush, but also to avoid having one or two children play so slowly that the rest of the group is forced to wait an inordinate amount of time.

Have each team sit down as its task is completed. The children can try to develop new balancing positions for the cup while they wait for the other teams to finish.

Have the children make suggestions about how and on what body part the cup could be balanced. In this activity a child must concentrate on the cup but still maintain an awareness of surrounding space. This is an important skill, and it is used to succeed in many sports.

MODIFICATIONS

You can have either the big or the small end of the cup touching the body part.

The children can crabwalk (on hands and feet with belly up) with the cup balanced on their stomachs.

Two teammates can carry the cup by pressing it between outside surfaces of their knees (requires a lot of skill and cooperation). The distance the cup is to be moved should be adjusted for difficulty.

Create an obstacle or obstacle course.

A toilet paper cardboard roll or other objects can be used instead of a cup.

For excitement add a few drops of water to the cup when it is being balanced on the head.

FALLING OFF THE LOG

This activity is similar to a tug-of-war except that there are only two players. Each player takes a position on a designated surface.

A rope is held between them, and each tries to pull the other off balance. Strategy and balance, rather than strength, are paramount. The player who remains on the surface longest becomes the defending champion and can be challenged by others for the title.

Perceptual motor development body control (balance); kinesthetic awareness; tactile awareness (see last statement in "Comments and Suggestions")

Attention span and concentration constant adapting; immediate feedback

Development of thinking processes constant monitoring and adapting; using additional input for decision making; using strategies to outwit opponent; self-evaluating

Physical abilities body control (adaptability, balance, coordination, counterbalance)

COMMENTS AND SUGGESTIONS

Several contests can be going on at once.
You may want to establish some local ground rules (e.g., don't jerk rope; don't wrap rope around hand; be careful rope is not wrapped around feet).
In some places this activity is played in a squatting position. Because of the most recent information concerning the potential danger to the knee when it is placed in greater than a forty-five degree angle with the body weight above it, this practice is strongly discouraged.
The sense of pressure on the bottoms of the feet (tactile), along with other sensory input, helps one to be aware of the change of balance and the need to adapt by shifting weight This sense can be improved by use and awareness.

This game can be played on the ground or floor with a designated area marked off in some way. It can also be played from a stable raised surface (tree stump, folded mats, board, cement blocks, old car tires, etc.).

This might be a good individual playground activity.

The distance between participants can vary in relation to the particular group and space available.

The skillful could turn around and work back to back or with closed eyes.

SQUIRREL IN THE TREE

Divide the group into threes ("Moving Math" might help, especially if the children are already familiar with it). Any leftover child will be an extra squirrel *without* a tree. In each group of three, two children will join hands and form a tree for the third child (the squirrel), who will stand between them. The leader will call "squirrels change trees." At this call all trees will raise their arms while the squirrels, including any extras, will scramble to find a new tree. If there are extra squirrels the challenge is to get to a free tree. If the group is even, the challenge is to do it as quickly as possible. Young children seem to enjoy the excitement of the process and who wins doesn't seem as important.

Perceptual motor development body and space relationships; estimation; directionality; motor planning; spatial awareness;

temporal awareness (moving speed of another); body control (balance and coordination)

Listening skills listening for call to move

Release of tension and excessive energy excitement; opportunity to move; some stretching; social interaction

Self-control dealing with excitement; making rapid decisions and adapting them if necessary

Development of thinking processes generating alternatives; decision making; adapting

Social growth working together; helping each other; awaiting turn

Physical abilities agility; ability to stop and start; adaptability

COMMENTS AND SUGGESTIONS

Cross Over might be a good preliminary activity (dodging, body control, responsibility for not bumping another).
If children enjoy this activity they might also like "Back to Back"and "Busy Bee".
There should be only one squirrel to a tree.
This might be a good outside game.

MODIFICATIONS

If your group needs an additional challenge, add a tagger (see "Safe from the Sharks").

CHAIN TAG

Partners hold hands or link elbows (see "Comments and Suggestions"). If the group is uneven allow a group of three. One pair is designated as "it." As this pair tags another pair, the two groups join together to be "it," and thus the chain continues to develop. A tag made when there is a break in the chain is not a legal tag.

Attention span and concentration challenge; group attachment; excitement

Release of tension opportunity to run

Self-control self-evaluation and decision making

Social growth accepting the right of each individual to play or stay out; working as a team

Physical fitness cardiorespiratory endurance; some shoulder girdle and arm development

COMMENTS AND SUGGESTIONS

It may help to establish some boundaries, such as lines on floor, plastic bottles, trees, ropes, end of grassy area. See if any natural boundaries can be established. I have found that understanding of the boundaries will occur as the children play.

It is good to play on grass or other soft substance, if available. Some children may not wish to hold hands at the beginning of this activity, so try to give choices (linked elbows; or you can also allow those who wish to stay out at the beginning to come in by linking with the chain of taggers whenever *they wish during* the activity). Usually after the game gets going, concern about personal contact is forgotten and everyone tends to hold hands or link elbows. I believe that choices make a positive contribution and that individual differences should be honored. I have also found that as I have become more comfortable with choices I have also become more creative in developing them, and I have been pleased with the results.

Consideration may need to be given to children at the end being whipped around or those in the center being pulled to discomfort. Maybe you could express this concern to the children and see what happens when they play. It may also be good to have an opportunity to leave the game. The leader, evaluating the need, might periodically blow a whistle to indicate a freeze. At each freeze, individuals who were fatigued or who desired to for any other reason could step out or step back in (by choice). This should be each child's choice and not evaluated by others.

Dropping out and coming in may require some group discussion and the development of an atmosphere conducive to respect for individual differences.

MODIFICATIONS

In limited space or with younger children, the runners go from one designated line to another on a signal. The taggers must remain connected. As children are caught they become part of the line. If the game is over too quickly, have the taggers disconnect and *sit* to tag. You may wish to add this variation to only the later part of the activity.

TOE FENCING

Players form groups of three (one referee and two fencers). Each player makes a fencing foil (see "Making Equipment at Little or No Cost," p. 201). Each group decides who will be its first referee. The two fencers face each other. On a predetermined signal, given by the leader, each fencer tries to *touch* the toes of the other fencer as many times as possible. The leader signals the end of the bout. The referee tries to determine who had the most legitimate touches. The referee and one fencer exchange roles in preparation for the next bout.

Perceptual motor development advanced body control; spatial awareness

Attention span and concentration pace; total involvement

Release of tension and excessive energy vigorous

Self-control controlled excitement

Development of thinking processes rapid decision making; thinking under stress; developing strategies

Physical abilities agility; dynamic balance; anticipation of another's move and responding accordingly

Physical fitness cardiovascular endurance; muscular endurance

For safety, have the fencers put the backs of their free hands to their foreheads. This position helps prevent heads from being banged together as the fencers bend forward to reach their opponents' toes.

The inclusion of a referee seems to add control to the activity. The referee can attempt to keep score (frequently impossible), place him- or herself between hazardous obstacles and the fencers, remind the fencers to maintain the safety position, and relieve one fencer during the next bout.

By having the third foil (referee's) made for each group, a broken foil is easily replaced.

You may wish to save the foils to reinforce and use for "Tall Sticks" ("Lumey Sticks" variation).

Stressing participation and fun may be more involving than stressing who won.

Thanks to Angela Morrison and Phil Gerney for introducing me to this activity.

MODIFICATIONS

This game can be played without foils. The hand is used for touches, which must be made on the outside of the knee (see also "Snatch the Flag").

APPENDIX A
61 ACTIVITIES THAT DEVELOP PERCEPTUAL MOTOR SKILLS

Perceptual abilities are vital to daily functioning. Planners of play are encouraged to continue learning more about perceptual motor development and to relate this knowledge to the selection of activities. For this reason, an outline of perceptual motor skills is presented here, followed by sixty-one activities that have been coded to this outline. For example, activities that develop and reinforce body awareness are coded with a 1, and activities that can contribute to body control and kinesthetic awareness in particular, are coded 3a.

1. Body awareness
2. Body image
3. Body control
   a. kinesthetic awareness
   b. balance
      (1) dynamic
      (2) static
   c. coordination
   d. reaction time
   e. movement time
   f. movement duplication
   g. adaptability (to need and purpose)
   h. object manipulation
4. Body and space relationships
   a. directionality
   b. laterality

5. Motor planning
6. Spatial awareness
   a. estimation
   b. relationships
7. Visual awareness
   a. acuity
   b. discrimination
   c. pattern recognition
   d. figure and ground
   e. depth perception
   f. tracking
   g. memory
8. Audio awareness
   a. acuity
   b. discrimination
   c. pattern recognition
   d. figure and ground
   e. directional perception
9. Temporal awareness
   a. discrimination
   b. pattern recognition
      (1) pace
      (2) rhythm
      (3) timing
      (4) sequencing
10. Tactile awareness

Activities are listed in the order in which they appear in this book. A more sophisticated breakdown of perceptual motor skills might be found in a text dealing specifically with perceptual motor development.

Cross Over   1, 3, 6
Cows and Ducks   3, 8a, d, e
Mirroring   1, 2, 3b, c, f, 4a, b, 5, 6a, b, 9b(1)
Follow Me   1, 2, 3c, f, 4a, b, 5, 7b, c
Body-Built Letters and Numbers   1, 2, 3c, 4, 5, 6, 7c

Sky Rider   1, 3a, g, 4, 9b(3)
Can You Do This?   4a, b
Creative Teeter-Totter   1, 3a, b, 6a, b
North, East, South, and West   6b
Lumey Sticks   3h, 7d, e, 9b(2), (4)
Swedish Meatball   3h, 4a, 6a, b, 7f
Monster's Choice   3b(1), 4a, b, 6a, b
Detective   7b, 8b
Solitary Ping-Pong   3h, 6, 7f, 9b(2), (3)
Snatch the Flag   3c, 4, 6a, b
Four Square   3h, 6, 7f
Zig Zag   8b
Crows and Cranes   3, 7b, 8b
Where Is It?   8e
Tiger, Tiger, Where's the Tiger?   8e
Gesture Name Game   5, 7b, c, 8b, c,
Unity Turns   3g, 4c
Jello Jiggle   1, 2, 3c
I Am a Balloon   1, 2, 3
Oh, MacDonald   1, 2
Back to Back   1, 6a, b
Busy Bee   1, 2, 6a, b
Crossed Wires   1, 2, 3c, g, 4b, 5
Team Juggle   3c, h, 4, 6a, 7d, f
Frantic Ball   3b, h, 4, 6a, b, 7d, f, 9b(1)
Beachball Volleyball   4, 6a, b, 7d, f, 9b(3)
Relaxing   2
Old Witchy-Toe Tag   1, 3, 6, 9b(1)
Safe from the Sharks   3g, 6, 9b(3)
Pass the Shoe   3h, 8c, 9b(3)
Fox and Squirrel   3c, h, 7f
Vampire   3a, 6
Streamers   4
Parts and Points   general and adaptable
Rhythms   3f, 8c

Paper Plate Play   2, 3, 4, 6
Memory Teaser Tester   7b, c, g
Shadows   2, 4, 6
Going On a Trip   3f
Clap Your Name   8b, c, d
Show Me the Time   3f, 4, 7c
Robot   3a, 5, 6
Cooperative Musical Chairs   4, 5, 6, 8a
Clothes Relay   1, 2, 3a, b, c, 6
All Aboard and Team on a T-Shirt   1, 3a, b
Big Turtle   4, 6b
Many Move   3f, 4, 5, 9b(3)
Trolley   9b(3)
Guard the Golden Fleece   3g, 5
African Simon Says   1, 3f, 7a
Carpet Activities   3a, b, c
Freeze   3a, b, 4, 6
Paper Cup Relay   1, 10
Falling Off the Log   3a, b, 10
Squirrel In the Tree   3b, c, 4, 5, 6, 9b(1)
Toe Fencing   1, 3a, b, c, d, e, g, 5, 6, 7f

APPENDIX B
24 ACTIVITIES THAT REINFORCE LEARNED INFORMATION

activity	information area
African Simon Says	pattern recognition
Wave the Ocean	left and right discrimination and laterality
I am a Balloon, Ping Pong Blow, and Paper Plate Play	concepts about air
North, East, South, and West	location and orientation
Show Me the Time	telling time
Moving Math	arithmetic
Magic Carpet	colors
Clap Your Name, Gesture Name Game	syllabic discrimination
Sounds Like	sound similarity and differences
Weather Walk	environmental studies
Taste and Smell	sensory studies (science)
Busy Bee, Can You Do This?	body parts
Crossed Wires, Pass the Shoe	tackling a problem
Car and Driver	right of way
Nine Square Hopscotch, True or False, Exchange Tag, Can You Do This?, and Body-Built Letters and Numbers	general; applicable to many areas

APPENDIX C
MAKING EQUIPMENT AT LITTLE OR NO COST

Making equipment is both fun and easy, and there are many values in having children participate in this process.

Since the materials are frequently things thrown away, the children have access to them, and their use may prove to be ecologically positive.

There is a sense of competency and pride that comes in making something yourself. Children can see the produced object as something they created.

After learning how to create a given piece of equipment, children can create additional ones, thus expanding their play opportunities. Several pieces are suitable for rainy-day play. Opportunities to improve eye-hand coordination, throwing ability, and other perceptual skills can become limitless.

The children can also create presents for younger brothers and sisters, thus having a source of giving and sharing.

Created equipment can be made to the size, softness, and weight that fits the individual user. This is not always possible with the mass-produced, standardized equipment.

Many of the pieces of equipment are safer than regular equipment. Items made of paper, yarn and cloth are generally softer and leave fewer bruises and other injuries.

Repairs and replacements are easy and immediate. A quick trip to the basement or trash starts the whole creative or re-creative process.

Poverty creates fewer limitations when equipment can be made. Do you remember when the game was called because the owner of the equipment went home?
Thinking up new ideas may allow for initiative and problem solving. It may also stimulate the creative process.

NYLON STOCKING AND COATHANGER RACKET

Materials needed:

wire coathanger
one leg of lady's hose
masking tape
scissors

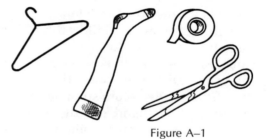

Figure A–1

Bend the coathanger into a rectangular or square shape. Straighten or bend the hook of the hanger to form a handle. Pull the foot of the hose over the top of the hanger (opposite the handle) and work down toward the handle. Pull so that a bouncy surface is formed. Wrap the hose leg around the handle to give some protection to the hand and tape the hose to the handle. Cut off any bulky excess.
Your students now have a lightweight racket that can be used somewhat like a badminton racket.

Figure A–2

Suggested Activities:

> hit to oneself
> hit to partner
> hit object tethered to overhead attachment
> create own activities

NEWSPAPER BAT; "TOE FENCING" FOILS OR "LUMEY STICKS"

Materials needed:

> newspaper
> tape

Figure A–3

For a bat, roll full sheets together, using enough sheets to make the bat sturdy but not heavy. For a toe fencing foil use about twelve full sheets. Since lumey sticks are made in various sizes, you will want to fold your newspaper accordingly before rolling.

It helps if you develop rolling techniques that finish with a fold rather than with many edges on the outside. A strip of masking tape around the top, bottom, and middle should make your equipment ready for use. Newsprint does come off on one's hands. If you choose, you can cover the handle area with other paper (such as magazine pages), cloth, spray paint, or tape. If not, be sure the children have access to soap and water.

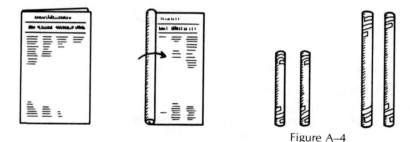

Figure A–4

BATTING TEE

Materials needed:
  several soda cans or tennis ball cans
  tape
  something like dirt or rocks (optional)
  whole cardboard box
  cutting tool for cardboard
  newspaper (optional)

Figure A–5

Tape cans together to approximately the waist height of your children. Place dirt or other material in the bottom can or two to give greater stability (optional). Cut a hole in the bottom of the cardboard box slightly smaller than the size of the can so that the can will have to be forced through the hole and thus will make a snug fit. Add newspaper to the box to add weight to the base if you wish.

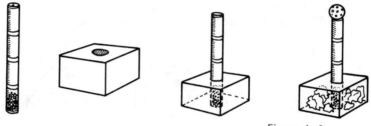

Figure A–6

PAPER WAD BALLS

Materials needed:

newspaper
    tape

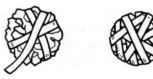

Figure A–7

Wad the newspaper into ball shape and tape.
Suggestions:

    Do not feel limited to only round balls. Children have formed a football shape in the same manner.
    Soccer balls are also a possibility.

Sponge-like sheets used in packing are sometimes available and are an excellent substitute for the newspaper.

SOCK BALLS

Materials needed:

old sock or single sock
newspaper or any stuffing material
rubber bands or needle and thread (optional)

Figure A–8

Stuff and shape the sock. Tuck in the excess material. Place rubber bands around the sock to hold in place or stitch it closed.

CARPET STRIPS

See "Carpet Activities"; size will vary with use.
Carpet scraps are frequently available without cost; check when new carpet is being laid. Tell your group what you are looking for and I'm sure they will find sources and resources for you. (Warning: You might be on the look out for anything that looks like it could be Mom's good hall runner.)

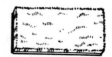

Figure A–9

YARN (FLEECE) BALLS

Materials needed:

scrap yarn
cardboard
cutting tool for cardboard
scissor or sharp cutting tool to cut through yarn
fishing line or strong string

Figure A–10

Cut out two donut-shaped patterns (approximately seven inches square) from cardboard. The hole should be roughly two and a half inches in diameter. Place the two donuts together and begin wrapping the yarn around the donut part of the pattern until the center hole is nearly filled. Since you will have to use smaller and smaller balls of scrap yarn to pass through the ever decreasing size of the center hole, you will have to have frequent knots.

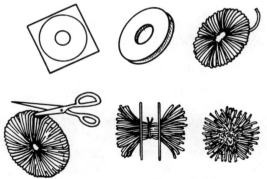

Figure A–11

These are no problem if tied securely. Next take a scissors or sharp tool and cut down between the two pieces of cardboard. Separate the pieces slightly and tie the yarn between them with strong line or string. Tie as tightly as possible and secure it with at least a double knot. Gently pull the cardboard off over the yarn. Fluff the yarn and shape with your scissors if your ball is not quite round.

Comments:

Heavy yarn or rug yarn wraps more quickly and makes good yarn balls.

Many people who knit have extra ends of scrap yarn in their knitting bags. Usually they are more than glad to donate to your cause. Also items can be unraveled to make useful yarn for balls. Children can help with this source.

This process requires time and patience.

You might want to try this item out yourself before trying it with children.

This might be an activity that you would want to do over a period of time.

You can purchase commercially made fleece or yarn balls from school equipment catalogs if you have more money than patience. This particular item is a very good piece of equipment if you must work in a small space or room used for other purposes.

INDOOR HOCKEY PUCKS

Materials needed:

old flat boxes of desired size
tape
newspaper cut to size of box (to give weight)

Using your newspaper bats as hockey sticks and one of these boxes as a puck, you can create some really enjoyable games, relays, and other activities.

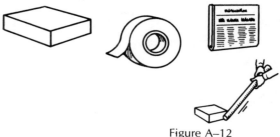

Figure A–12

STREAMERS

Materials needed:

> crepe paper (rolls or package)
> scissors

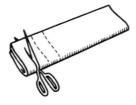 

Figure A–13

If you are using package crepe paper, cut strips approximately two to three inches wide. Make them long enough so that each child can successfully create a circular pattern as the streamer is moved through the air. You now have an individual activity, or you can add music and group formations and patterns. (When I was twelve years old I saw over two hundred boy scouts moving red, white, and blue streamers to "America the Beautiful"; it was very impressive.)

This activity should help keep shoulders well aligned. Try to encourage the children to use both arms and backward as well as forward arm circles. This allows for symmetrical development and the stretching of chest muscles.

VALUES OF SPECIFIC
ACTIVITIES FOR
CHILDREN

	①	②	③	④	⑤	⑥	⑦	⑧	⑨	⑩
	perceptual motor development	attention span/concentration	listening skills	release of tension/excessive energy	self-control	development of thinking processes	reinforcement of learned information	social growth	physical abilities	physical fitness

● activity can make a major contribution in this area

• activity has the potential to contribute in this area

page	activity	①	②	③	④	⑤	⑥	⑦	⑧	⑨	⑩
181	African Simon Says	•	•			•	•			●	•
166	Alaskan Baseball		•			•	•		●	•	
162	All Aboard (Team on a T-Shirt)	•			•	•	●		●	•	
110	Animal Walks		•	•	•	•	●	•		•	•
141	Arrows	●	•		•	•	●	•		•	
72	Back to Back	•	●	●	●	●	•			•	•
82	Beachball Volleyball	•	•	•	●	•				•	•
53	Beep	•	•	●		•					
164	Big Turtle	●	•			•	•		●		
38	Birds Fly			●	•	•	•	•			•
12	Body-Built Letters and Numbers	●				•	•	●		•	
72	Busy Bee	•	●	•	●	●	•			•	
16	Can You Do This?	●	•	•	●		●	●		●	
160	Car and Driver	•	•		•	●			●		
182	Carpet Activities	•			●				•	●	●
182	Carpet Skiing	•			●				•	●	•
191	Chain Tag		•		●	•					●
125	Changing Ends (The Uneven Boxes)						●		●		
134	Clap Your Name	●	•	●		•	•	●	•		
157	Clothes Relay	•			●	•	•		●		
153	Cooperative Musical Chairs	•		•	•	•	•		●		
153	Cooperative Musical Hoops		•	•	●	●	•		●		
7	Cows and Ducks	●	•	●	•	•					
18	Creative Teeter-Totter	●	●			•	●	•	•	●	
74	Crossed Wires	●	•		•	•		•	•	●	
5	Cross Over	●	•	•	•	●	•			●	●
49	Crows and Cranes	●	●	●	•	•	●			•	•
34	Detective	•	●	●		•	•				
177	Egg Blow		•		•				•		●
138	Exchange Tag		•		•	•		•	●	•	
187	Falling Off the Log	●	•			•	•			●	
10	Follow Me	●	●		•	•	•	•		●	
43	Four Square	●	●		•	•			●	●	
97	Fox and Squirrel	•	●		●	●	●			•	•
78	Frantic Ball	●	●		●	•	•			●	•

		1	2	3	4	5	6	7	8	9	10
184	Freeze	●	•		•	•	•			●	
58	Gesture Name Game	•	•	●	•		●	•		•	
126	Going On a Trip	•	●	•	•		●			•	
81	Gotcha	•	•		●	•				•	
176	Guard the Golden Fleece	•	●		●		•			●	
151	Happy Landing	●	●	●		•	•		●	●	
159	Human Knot		•		•	•	•		●		
66	I Am A Balloon	•	●	•	●	•	•	•	•	•	
82	Infinity Volleyball	●	•		●	•		•		•	
65	Jello Jiggle	•	•	•	●	•	•			●	
119	Line Tag		●				●			●	●
70	Lion Hunt		●	•	●	•	•			•	
123	Lion, Hunter, Gun		•	•	●	●	●		•	•	
180	Loo K'Bah Zee		•							●	
25	Lumey Sticks	●	●			•	•		●	●	
143	Magic Carpet			•	•	•	•	●	•	•	
168	Many Move	•	•			•	•		●	•	
8	Me and My Shadow	●	●		•	•	•			•	
117	Memory Teaser Tester	•	•				●				
8	Mirroring	●	●		•	●	•		●	●	
30	Monster's Choice	•	●		●	●	•	•	●		•
110	Mood Walks	•	•	•	●	•	●	•	•		
155	Moving Boxes		•			•	●		●		
136	Moving Math		•	•	•	•	•	●			•
145	Nine Square Hopscotch	•	•		•	•	•	●		•	•
19	North, East, South and West (orientation)	●	•	●	•		●	●			
69	Oh, MacDonald	•	•	•	●	•			●		•
90	Old Witchy-Toe Tag	●	•		●	●	•		●	●	
186	Paper Cup Relay	●	•			•			•	●	
112	Paper Plate Play	•			•	•	●	•	•	•	•
113	Partner Tag		•		•	•	●		•	•	
102	Parts and Points	•	•	•	•	●	•				
94	Pass the Shoe	•	•	•		●	•		•	•	
177	Ping-Pong Blow					•			•		●
56	Prowling Tigers	●	•	●		•					
32	Push or Pull		•		●				•	•	•
89	Relaxing	•	•		●	●	•			•	●
104	Rhythms	•	●	•		●	•		•	•	
151	Robot	●	●	●		•	•		●	•	
92	Safe From the Sharks	•	•	•	●	●	•		•	•	
120	Shadow Plays	•	•		•	•	●		•	•	
120	Shadows	•	•		•	•	●		•	•	
141	Show Me the Time	•	•	•	•		●	●		•	•
38	Simon Says		●	●	●	•	●				•
14	Sky Rider	●	•		•	•			●	●	•
32	Snatch the Bacon		●	•			•			●	